HOW TO MAKE AND DECORATE

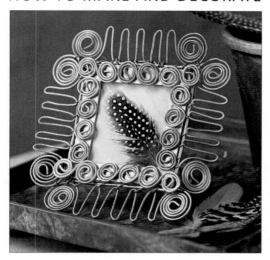

30 FABULOUS
PICTURE FRAMES

HOW TO MAKE AND DECORATE
30 FABULOUS PICTURE FRAMES

A practical and fun guide to making and personalizing a variety
of picture frames with creative and stunning decorative effects

Beautifully illustrated with over 340 inspirational photographs,
with step-by-step instructions for every project

Contributing Editor: Simona Hill

southwater

This edition is published by Southwater, an imprint of Anness Publishing Ltd, Blaby Road, Wigston, Leicestershire LE18 4SE; info@anness.com

www.southwaterbooks.com; www.annesspublishing.com

If you like the images in this book and would like to investigate using them for publishing, promotions or advertising, please visit our website www.practicalpictures.com for more information.

A CIP catalogue record for this book is available from the British Library.

Publisher: Joanna Lorenz
Editorial Director: Helen Sudell
Editors: Simona Hill and Elizabeth Woodland
Copy Editors: Beverley Jollands and Heather Haynes
Designer: Nigel Partridge
Production Controller: Mai-Ling Collyer

Previously published as part of a larger volume, *The Complete Book of Picture Framing & Decorative Framework*

Disclaimer

Protective clothing should be worn when performing some of the tasks described in this book. Wear rubber (latex) gloves for grouting and using glass etching paste; wear protective gloves and goggles when cutting glass, breaking mosaic tesserae with a hammer or tile nippers, or cutting wire or sheet metal. Wear a face mask when sawing, sanding or drilling medium density fibreboard, working with powdered grout or using solvent-based sprays.

Every effort has been made to ensure the project instructions are accurate. The author and publisher cannot accept liability for any resulting damage or loss to persons or property as a result of carrying out any of the projects. Before you begin any project you should be sure and confident that you understand the instructions.

Contents

Introduction   6

Cardboard, Paper, Tin and Wire   **8**
Paper Materials and Equipment   10
Metal Materials and Equipment   11
Techniques   12
Corrugated Picture Frame   16
Starry Cardboard Frame   17
Seaside Papier Mâché Mirror   18
Hammered Paper Frame   19
Oranges and Lemons Decoupage   20
Swirly Mirror   22
Ivy Leaf Frame   24
Punched Tin Leaf Frame   26
Wire Picture Frame   28
Metal Foil Frame   30
Painted Tinware Mirror   32
Zigzag Wire Frame   34

Flowers, Beads and Fabric   **36**
Materials and Equipment   38
Techniques   40
Poppy Seedhead Frames   44
Pressed-Leaf Frame   46
Artificial Flower Mirror Frame   47
String Spirals Frame   48

Bead-Encrusted Frames   50
Sequins and Beads   52
Flowered Frame   54
Padded Silk Picture Frame   56
Ribbonwork Frame   58
Fun Felt Frame   60
Plastic Fantastic   62

Plaster, Clay and Mosaic   **64**
Plaster and Clay Materials   66
Plaster and Clay Equipment   67
Mosaic Materials and Equipment   68
Techniques   69
Plaster Cast Frame   72
Geometric Clay Frames   74
Modelled Flower Garden Frame   76
Modelled Lizard Mirror Frame   78
Stitched Clay Frame   81
Mediterranean Mirror   84
Valentine Mirror   86
Grotto Frame   88
Rock Pool Mirror   90

Templates   92
Acknowledgements   95
Index   96

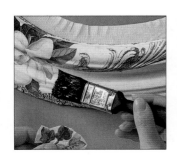   

Introduction

Creating beautiful and exciting frames is a pleasure that anyone can enjoy. They can be as simple or as complex as you like, and with so many different materials to choose from the only limiting factor is likely to be your imagination.

You can frame just about anything – a photograph or painting, a mirror, or virtually any object that takes your fancy – and transform it into something good enough to fit into the style of your home. Sometimes the simplest styles create the most striking effect, while wilder creations may become a work of art in their own

right. Whatever you choose to do, the style should always suit the image or object being framed. There are 32 easy-to-follow projects to help you get started with this rewarding activity, with projects to suit every taste –

traditional, rustic, modern, ornamental – and every level of expertise, from novice to experienced.

The first chapter is devoted to such seemingly unlikely raw materials as paper, cardboard, tin and wire, which can all be formed into fantastic frames.

In the second chapter you will learn how you can create textured frames by applying eye-catching materials like dried flowers, leaves and seed heads, or beautiful fabrics such as silk, beads and sequins. In the third chapter you can find out how more challenging materials such as plaster, clay and mosaics can be skilfully manipulated to produce some quite remarkable results.

Each chapter starts off with detailed information about the materials used and the techniques and tools required for getting the best out of them. Every project has been graded according to the level of skill required to complete it: the simplest, suitable for a complete beginner to start with, are

marked with a single symbol; while a marking of five symbols indicates that a more advanced level of skill is required. Once you have mastered the basic techniques, you will find that you can easily adapt the projects to suit your own style and taste, or those of your friends and family, and you will then be ready to embark on a truly creative experience.

Cardboard, Paper, Tin and Wire

You can make unusual and innovative frames from the most basic materials, and, in many cases, you need look no further than paper and cardboard. Cardboard is strong enough to form a rigid structure, which can then be inventively decorated with paper or paint. Use coils of galvanized wire for intricate frame edgings, or stamp sheet metal with a nail or centre punch to make decorative embossed patterns in both traditional and modern styles.

Both cardboard and paper are everyday materials and are easily available to buy, but also look at every piece of packaging that comes into your home: much of it will prove useful for making frames.

Paper Materials and Equipment

Medium density fibreboard (MDF)
Supplied in various thicknesses, it is cheap and easy to shape.

Newspaper
Tear with the grain to make neat strips for papier mâché.

Packaging
Recycle packaging materials, such as egg cartons and cereal boxes.

PVA (white) glue
Use diluted to soak paper for papier mâché. It dries clear and forms a waterproof coating so it can be used to strengthen and seal paper.

Tape
Use for temporary fixings and to mask painted areas or protect mirrors. Use gummed tape to bind cardboard.

Brown parcel wrap
Makes very strong papier mâché. Its matt surface takes paint well.

Cardboard
Available in many thicknesses. Cut with a craft knife on a cutting mat.

Corrugated cardboard and paper
Double-walled corrugated cardboard is rigid and makes a strong basic structure. Single-walled corrugated paper is flexible and decorative.

Decorative paper
Use handmade, metallic or marbled papers and printed wrapping paper. For collages, try old manuscript.

Dutch metal leaf
Imitation metal leaf is easy to apply. Varnish the surface when complete.

Liquidizer
For breaking down paper fibres to make papier mâché pulp. Do not use the same machine to process food.

Tissue paper
Available in many colours for collage and decoupage.

Varnish and sealant
Oil-based and acrylic varnishes are available. Shellac and sanding sealer add strength to papier mâché and cardboard constructions.

Wallpaper paste
Add to papier mâché pulp to strengthen the mixture.

All the wire and sheet metal you will need to make the projects in this chapter are widely available from hardware and craft suppliers. Invest in the correct cutters and pliers to make shaping metal simple.

Metal Materials and Equipment

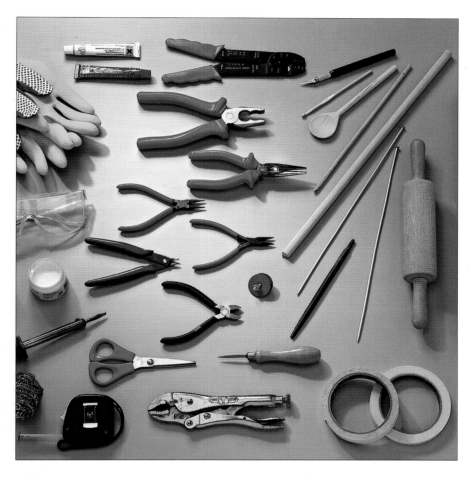

Metal foil
Craft aluminium and copper foil comes in a range of thicknesses. It is very soft and easy to fold and cut.

Pliers
Use parallel (channel-type) pliers for holding wire and metal and long- or snub-nosed pliers for curling wire and

Protective clothing
Wear leather gloves and a work shirt when working with wire or cutting metal. Wear a mask when soldering or using solvent-based sprays.

Soldering iron, solder and flux
A soldering iron is used to join pieces of metal using solder, a metal alloy with a low melting point. Flux is used to keep the metal surface clean.

Tin plate
Tin plate has a very bright surface and will not tarnish.

Tin snips (shears)
For cutting sheet metal and foil.

Wire
Galvanized wire is hard and does not rust. Aluminium and copper wire are very soft and easy to work with. Use fine-gauge wire to bind thicker wire coils in place. Chicken wire makes a decorative backing for wire frames.

Ballpoint pen
The ballpoint tip is used to incise designs in soft metal foils. Using an old pen without ink keeps the work clean.

Bottle caps
Colourful bottle caps can be used decoratively, nailed to a frame or threaded on wire.

Brass and copper pins
Use decorative large-headed pins to attach metal sheet to a wooden frame.

Broomstick
Used for making large coils in wire.

Centre punch
Used for decorating sheet metal.

Chipboard
Place a spare piece of chipboard under the metal sheet before using a punch.

Lead strip
Self-adhesive lead strip is soft and flexible. Cut with a sturdy craft knife.

Techniques using paper, cardboard, tin and wire open up a whole range of creative opportunities, enabling you to make and decorate a variety of unusual frames using easily obtainable materials.

Techniques

Making paper pulp

Paper pulp is an adaptable material that is easy to model into frames. The basic mixture can be strengthened by adding white interior filler or wallpaper paste, and made more flexible with a little linseed oil.

1 Tear the paper into postage-stamp-sized pieces. Soak the paper scraps in water for at least 2 hours.

2 Place a handful of torn paper in a liquidizer and fill two-thirds full with water. Liquidize briefly to a pulp.

3 Pour the batch of pulp through a sieve and squeeze out as much moisture as possible.

Papier mâché

Tear along the grain of the newspaper to produce long straight strips of paper and soak in dilute PVA (white) glue. Several layers of papier mâché can be used to reinforce cardboard frames and other structures.

1 Grasp several folded sheets of newspaper in one hand, and begin a tear about 2.5cm/1in from the edge. Pull directly down, and the paper will tear into long, straight strips.

2 Soak the strips in PVA (white) glue, and lay them overlapping on the cardboard. Apply five layers of strips, adding each at right angles to the layer beneath for extra strength.

3 When the glue is dry, rub the surface with fine sandpaper (glasspaper) to smooth it and disguise the edges of the paper strips. Wear a protective face mask when sanding.

Decoupage This technique enables you to create beautiful and unique decorations on your picture frames. All you need is skill with a pair of scissors and some paper motifs.

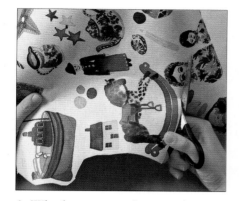

1 Whether you prefer to use a pair of scissors or a craft knife, the basic principles remain the same. Always use a cutting mat with a craft knife. Use a large pair of scissors to cut around the outer edge of the motif. Then use small scissors to trim around the edges.

2 You can paint the motifs before cutting them out. Dilute artist's acrylic paints with a little water, mix the colours and test them on scrap paper. When you are satisfied with the colours, lightly shade in the pale areas of the paper cut-outs, then move on to the darker areas, increasing the intensity of colour.

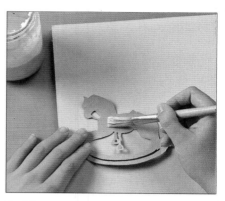

3 Using an artist's brush, spread diluted PVA (white) glue on the wrong side of the cut-out. Thinly cover the entire surface right up to the edge. Alternatively, brush the glue on to the surface of the frame, especially when gluing a fairly large or intricate piece. Remove any surplus glue while it is still wet with a damp cloth.

4 Press the cut-out gently on to the surface, starting at the centre and working outwards. If you are working on a small item, hold your work up to the light to highlight any imperfections. Lift any edges that have been missed and dab on some glue. Leave the decoupage for a few minutes, then, using a barely moistened sponge, gently wipe away excess glue from around the motif. Leave to dry.

5 If your decoupage design has a cut-out border with corners, you will need to cut the borders so that they are slightly longer than the edges. Mark the centre point of each edge lightly with a pencil. Centre the border, using the pencil mark as a guide, and stick down the centre portion of the border only, leaving the ends free. Do the same with all the remaining edges.

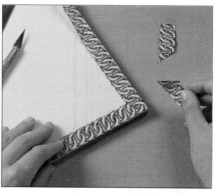

6 Place a metal ruler at 45° across the angle where two sections of the border overlap, ensuring that the ruler lines up with the corner. Using a craft knife, cut through both borders at once. Lift off the surplus paper, then glue down the mitred corners.

Wire Coils are probably the most commonly used decorative devices in wire-work. They also have a practical use as they neaten and make safe what would otherwise be sharp ends, while adding grace and style.

Closed coils

Using round-nosed (snub-nosed) pliers, make a small loop at the end of the wire. Hold the loop firmly with parallel (channel-type) pliers, and use them to bend the wire around until you have a coil of the size required.

Open coils

Using round-nosed (snub-nosed) pliers, make a small loop at the end of the wire. Holding the loop in the pliers, place your thumb against the wire and draw the wire across it to form a curve. Use your eye to judge the space left between the rings of the coil. Finally, flatten the coil.

Flattened extended coils

1 Wrap the wire several times around a broomstick or other cylindrical object to make a coil. If you are using galvanized wire, you will need to brace your thumb firmly against it.

2 After removing the coil from the broomstick, splay out the loops one by one, holding them firmly between your fingers and thumbs.

Safety advice

• A heavy work shirt and protective leather gloves should always be worn when handling either cut metal pieces or uncut sheet metal.

• Tin shears and snips are strong enough to cut through fairly heavy metal, and are very sharp. They should be handled with respect and, like all other tools, should always be kept in a safe place, well away from children, both during and after use.

• Clean up as you work. Collect small shards of tin together as you cut and make sure you don't leave any on the floor where people and animals might walk on them.

• A protective face mask and goggles should be worn during soldering as the hot metal, solder and flux give off fumes. Work should be carried out on a soldering mat and the iron placed on a metal rest when not in use.

• Soldering should always be carried out in a well-ventilated area. Don't lean too near your work during soldering to avoid close contact with fumes.

• Wear protective gloves when soldering, as the soldering iron and metal tend to get very hot.

Metal   Punching is one of the most common methods of decorating tin. A centre punch or nail, plus a ball hammer, are used to produce the knobbly patterns, either on the front or back of the tin.

Getting the design right

If you want to emboss a sophisticated pattern, draw the design out first on a sheet of graph paper and punch through the paper into the tin, following the lines. The graph paper should be taped to the tin, and the tin attached to a piece of chipboard using panel pins (brads) to keep it steady as you punch.

Punching tin from the front

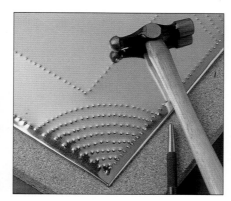

If a design is punched into tin from the front, the resulting pattern will be indented. If it is punched from the back, the pattern will be raised. If an area of tin is punched from the front, and the indentations are made very close together, the punched area recedes and the unpunched area becomes slightly raised.

Punching tin from the back

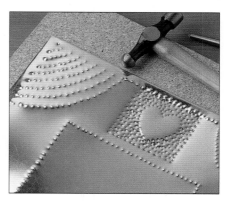

Punching a pattern into a piece of tin from the back leaves a very pleasing knobbly effect on the surface of the tin. Patterns can be applied with punches or nails of different sizes to make a dotty texture. Short lines can be made using a small chisel. It is also possible to buy decorative punches that have designs engraved on the tip.

Embossing aluminium foil

Aluminium foil can easily be cut and folded, so it is useful for cladding frames. Its softness makes it very easy to emboss by drawing on to the back of the foil using an empty ballpoint pen, which produces a raised design on the other side.

Cutting tin

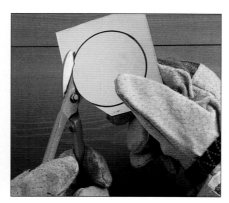

If you are cutting a small intricate shape from sheet tin, tin snips are easier to manage than shears. Don't attempt to turn the snips around in the metal: cut as far as you can, then remove the snips and turn the metal before continuing.

Corrugated paper can look stunning when used innovatively. It is easy to work with but crushes easily. To avoid this problem and create a different look, flatten the ridges with a ruler before you begin work.

Corrugated Picture Frame

you will need
metal ruler
pencil
corrugated cardboard
craft knife
cutting mat
fine corrugated paper in
different colours
scissors
PVA (white) glue and brush

1 Measure the image to be framed and decide on the size and shape of frame required. Draw the frame backing on to corrugated cardboard and cut it out using a craft knife and metal ruler.

2 Use the backing as a template to draw and cut out the front of the frame from coloured corrugated paper. Using the image as a guide, mark and carefully cut out the central frame area.

3 Make a stand for the frame from cardboard and glue in place on the back. Decorate the front with twisted strips of coloured paper. Glue the image in place so that the backing colour shows through in a thin border all round. Stick the frame together.

Plain brown parcel wrap is an ideal material for papier mâché, and its warm tones produce a stylish, natural look. This frame, with its low-relief pattern, exploits the material's qualities in a simple design.

Starry Cardboard Frame

you will need

metal ruler

T-square

pencil

thick corrugated cardboard

cutting mat

craft knife

tracing paper

strong, clear glue

lightweight corrugated cardboard

PVA (white) glue

paintbrush

sheet of plastic

brown parcel wrap

masking tape

picture hanger

1 From thick corrugated cardboard cut a 38cm/15in square for the frame. Cut out an 18cm/7in square from the centre. Cut out eight stars using the template provided, and four circles from cardboard. Glue the circles to four stars. Glue the stars to the frame. Put the plain ones at the corners.

2 Cut a backing board and a frame spacer from lightweight cardboard. Prime all the pieces with diluted PVA (white) glue. Leave to dry. Glue the spacer to the back of the frame. Tear wide strips of brown paper and dip them into the diluted glue. Cover the frame and backing with two layers.

3 When the papier mâché is dry, glue the covered backing board to the frame, lining up the edges accurately. Hold the frame together with masking tape and seal the bottom and side edges with two layers of papier mâché strips. When dry, glue a hanger to the back with clear glue.

Decorated with glass droplets, this marine-inspired mirror is made of moulded papier mâché. The wave-like frame is cut from cardboard, then covered with paper pulp to build up its organic form.

Seaside Papier Mâché Mirror

you will need
strong cardboard
craft knife
cutting mat
newspaper
wallpaper paste
PVA (white) glue and brush
paintbrush
acrylic primer: white
glass droplets
epoxy resin glue
gouache paints: deep yellow, cadmium yellow, deep cobalt, pale blue, green, red, indigo and white
artist's paintbrushes
enamel paint: gold
clear gloss and matt varnishes
mirror and fixing tabs
plate-hanging fixture
screwdriver

Papier mâché pulp (see Techniques)
newspaper
2 tablespoons PVA (white) glue
1 tablespoon linseed oil
few drops oil of cloves
2 tablespoons wallpaper paste

1 Enlarge the template at the back of the book on a photocopier. Transfer it to the cardboard and cut out using a craft knife and working on a cutting mat. Make the paper pulp by mixing all the ingredients together and apply this to the cardboard, to build up a three-dimensional form. Allow to dry.

2 Cover the whole frame with three to four layers of newspaper, soaked in wallpaper paste. Allow to dry. Coat with PVA (white) glue, then with acrylic primer. When this is dry, attach the glass droplets using epoxy resin glue. Decorate with gouache paints and add detail with the gold paint.

3 Paint the frame with several coats of gloss varnish, adding matt varnish in places to provide contrast. Allow the varnish to dry between each coat. Secure the mirror with mirror fixing-tabs. Finally, attach the plate-hanging fixture, securing all screws with epoxy resin glue.

This delicate frame is created using a plastic light switch surround as a mould. The mottled cream pulp is made from two shades of scrap paper and is applied to create a deliberately irregular shape.

Hammered Paper Frame

you will need

white and cream paper scraps

liquidizer

sieve

cloth

plastic light switch plate

cream or pearl beads

spoon

sponge

small hammer

PVA (white) glue

container for diluting glue

glue brush

tea or brown watercolour paint

artist's paintbrush

1 Mixing both colours of paper, make the scrap paper into pulp (see Techniques). Drain it through a sieve and squeeze out the excess moisture.

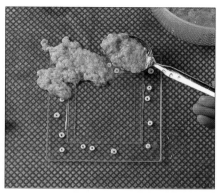

2 Smooth out a cloth on a flat waterproof surface, then put the light switch plate face down on top. Arrange the beads randomly on the plastic surface. Spoon pulp over the beads and the light switch plate, allowing it to spread over the edges of the plate. Sponge the pulp gently to remove any excess water.

3 Press a small hammer randomly into the wet pulp to make a textured border. Leave to dry, then remove the mould. Seal with diluted PVA (white) glue (equal parts glue and water). For an antique effect, stain the frame with tea or brown watercolour paint.

This striking papier mâché frame is decorated with decoupage motifs of oranges and lemons. Hunt around for interesting wrapping paper with clear and colourful images.

Oranges and Lemons Decoupage

you will need

corrugated cardboard

craft knife

metal ruler

cutting mat

mirror, 15 x 18cm/6 x 7in

wallpaper paste

paintbrushes

newspaper

acrylic paints: black, yellow and green

artist's brush

paper clip (fastener)

acrylic gesso

natural sponge

wrapping paper

scraps of printed paper or manuscript

white tissue paper

matt acrylic varnish

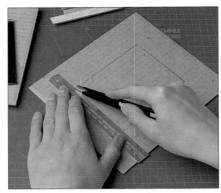

1 Cut two 17 x 20cm/6½ x 8in rectangles from corrugated cardboard using a craft knife and metal ruler and working on a cutting mat. Centre the mirror on one piece and cut spacer strips of cardboard to fit around it down two sides and across the bottom. Cut a window out of the centre of the other rectangle of cardboard, leaving a 4cm/1½ in border.

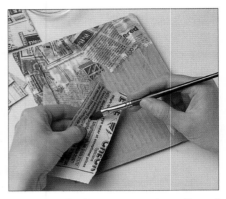

2 Coat all the pieces of cardboard with wallpaper paste. Leave to dry. Tear the newspaper into strips and coat them with paste. Cover the front of the frame with the newspaper. Paste the spacer strips in position on the sides and bottom of the back panel. Cover with papier mâché strips and leave to dry. Apply a second layer.

3 When the papier mâché is dry, paint the inside surfaces of the frame black to minimize any possible reflection they might give in the mirror.

4 Open out the paper clip (fastener) and thread one end through the papier mâché at the centre back of the frame. Paste strips of newspaper over the clip, leaving the top section showing to act as a hook.

5 Join the front of the frame to the back with more strips of pasted newspaper. For added strength, paste folded strips over the top of the frame to each side of the opening. Once dry, paint the frame with acrylic gesso.

6 Sponge the entire frame with thin yellow paint, then with green paint to create an all-over mottled effect.

7 Tear the motifs from the wrapping paper in interesting shapes and arrange them over the frame surface. Fill the gaps between the motifs with small pieces of printed paper. Paste in position.

8 Soften the design by tearing small pieces of white tissue paper and pasting them on to the frame. When the paste is dry, paint the frame with two coats of matt varnish and insert the mirror into the top slit to finish.

A plain mirror frame made from medium density fibreboard becomes a work of art when decorated with strips of wrapping paper. Apply crackle varnish and gold powder to give the frame a rich texture.

Swirly Mirror

you will need

mirror tile

pencil

medium density fibreboard (MDF),
8mm/⅓in thick

metal ruler

jigsaw

protective mask

wood glue

wrapping paper

craft knife

cutting mat

PVA (white) glue

felt-tipped pen

spray adhesive

two-stage crackle varnish

paintbrushes

gold powder

soft cloth

spray fixative

clear oil-based varnish

drill with wood drill bits

string

adhesive fixer pads

picture rings and chain

screwdriver

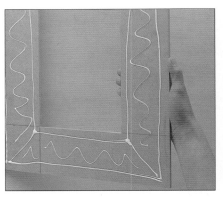

1 Draw around the mirror tile on to medium density fibreboard (MDF) and add a 9cm/3½in border all around. Wearing a mask, cut a back and a front panel to this size using a jigsaw. Cut out the centre of the front panel. Cut a plaque measuring 8.5 x 18cm/3¼ x 7in. Glue the panels together using wood glue.

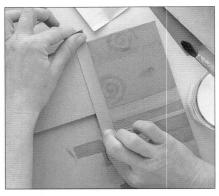

2 Cut strips of wrapping paper in varying widths using a craft knife, ruler and cutting mat and arrange them on the frame front. Glue in place using PVA (white) glue.

3 To cover the corners, place a piece of wrapping paper on the frame and press around the edges. Remove and cut away the corner section. Glue the corner in place.

4 Using the template provided, draw two decorative swirls on the back of another paper using a felt-tipped pen. Cut out the swirls and spray the back of each with adhesive. Glue on to two corners of the frame.

5 Apply two thin coats of crackle varnish, following the manufacturer's instructions to give a craquelure finish to the frame.

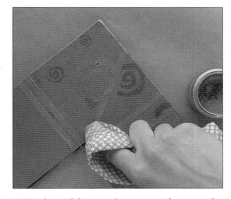

6 Rub gold powder into the cracks with a cloth, using small amounts at a time. Rub off any excess. Seal the frame with fixative. Decorate the hanging plaque in the same way as the frame. Coat both the frame and the hanging plaque with varnish.

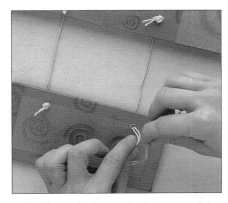

7 Drill two holes in the bottom of the frame and in the top of the hanging plaque. Join together with string.

8 Stick the mirror in place using adhesive fixer pads.

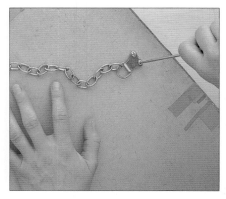

9 Attach the picture rings and chain to the back of the frame.

Although this design looks handpainted, it is in fact created using motifs cut from paper table napkins. Classical borders and creamy white flowers combine with the ivy to decorate a very elegant frame.

Ivy Leaf Frame

you will need

masking tape

wooden frame, prepared and sanded, with oval mirror

paintbrushes

primer: white

emulsion (latex) paint: white

black-and-white paper borders

small scissors

wallpaper paste

pasting brush

white paper napkins with ivy leaf design

scissors

cream or white floral motifs

water-based varnish

two-step crackle varnish

hairdryer, optional

oil paint: raw umber

soft white cloths

white spirit (paint thinner)

oil-based varnish

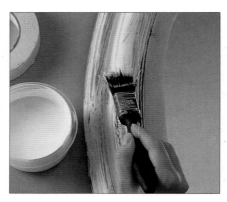

1 Place masking tape around the edge of the mirror glass to protect it. Apply two coats of primer to the frame, followed by a coat of white emulsion (latex) paint. Allow the paint to dry between each coat.

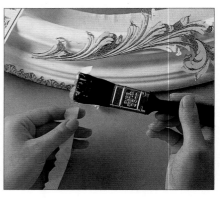

2 Using a copyright-free border design, photocopy and cut out enough lengths to go round the outer and inner edges of the frame. Using wallpaper paste, apply the borders to the frame in small sections, aligning and joining up the design as necessary.

3 Remove the second, unprinted layer of tissue from the back of each napkin. Cut around the ivy shapes, leaving a narrow border of plain tissue.

4 Cut out floral motifs in the same way. Apply more paste to the mirror frame and stick the ivy trails and flowers in place. Allow to dry.

5 Apply several coats of water-based varnish to protect the design. Leave to dry between each coat. Following the manufacturer's instructions, brush on a thin, even layer of the first stage of the crackle varnish. Leave for 1–3 hours until tacky.

6 Brush on two coats of the second stage of the varnish, the second coat 30 minutes after the first, and leave to dry completely. If necessary, encourage the cracks to appear by moving a hairdryer, on its lowest setting, over the varnished surface.

7 Apply a small quantity of raw umber paint to a soft cloth. Add a little white spirit (paint thinner). Apply to the frame using a circular motion then, with a clean cloth, rub over the surface to remove the excess paint. The colour will remain in the cracks. Apply six to ten coats of oil-based varnish to protect the surface.

Tin is a soft metal that can be decorated easily using a centre punch or a blunt chisel to create dots and lines. Keep your punched design graphic and uncluttered, as too much fine detail will get lost.

Punched Tin Leaf Frame

you will need

wide, flat wooden frame
thin cardboard
felt-tipped pen
scissors
adhesive tape
sheet of tin
centre punch
hammer
tin snips (shears)
protective gloves (optional)
chisel
ridged paint scraper
copper nails
metal polish and cloth, optional
clear varnish and brush, optional
paper towels and salt water, optional
wax and soft cloth, optional

1 Place the wooden frame on a piece of thin cardboard and draw around the outline with a felt-tipped pen. Add borders at the outside and centre edges to allow for turnings, and cut out the template with scissors. Tape the template on to a sheet of tin. Mark the corners using a centre punch and hammer, and mark the straight lines with the felt-tipped pen.

2 Cut out the shape with tin snips. (You may want to wear protective gloves to protect your hands from the tin's sharp edges.) Using a hammer and chisel, cut through the centre of the frame in a diagonal line, then use tin snips to cut along the remaining sides, to leave you with a cut-out square, a little smaller than the centre of the frame.

3 Place the wooden frame on the tin and use a ridged paint scraper to coax the metal up the sides of the frame.

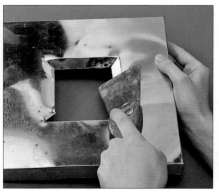

4 Turn the frame over and push down the metal edges in the centre, again using the ridged paint scraper.

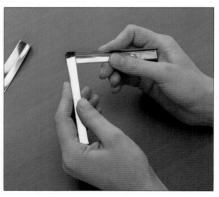

5 Cut two strips of tin, each 20cm x 18mm/8 x ¾in. Snip at the halfway mark and fold at a 90° angle. Nail the strips to the inner edge of the frame, using copper nails.

6 Carefully hammer copper nails along the outer edges of the frame so that the tin is firmly secured in place.

7 Draw a freehand leaf or other design on the tin frame with a felt-tipped pen, remembering to keep the pattern simple and bold for the best effect. Any errors can be easily wiped away from the metal surface.

8 Press the leaf design on to the tin in dots, using a hammer and centre punch. Alternatively, a blunt chisel and hammer can be used to press the design on to the tin in straight lines.

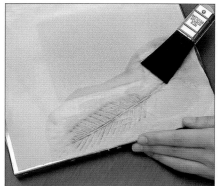

9 There are two ways to finish the frame. Clean the tin with metal polish and a soft cloth, removing any traces of marker pen. To preserve the finish, seal with clear varnish.

10 To rust the frame, cover with a paper towel and dampen with salt water. Keep the paper damp until the frame has rusted (2–7 days). Remove the paper and seal with wax when dry.

This light and airy picture frame is made from thick aluminium wire, which is soft and bends easily to form the filigree frame surround. The pastel ribbon and old-fashioned picture create a Victorian look.

Wire Picture Frame

you will need

round-nosed (snub-nosed) pliers

soft aluminium wire, 3mm/⅛in and 1mm/½₅in thick

ruler

wire cutters

small-gauge chicken wire

gloves, optional

galvanized wire, 1.5mm/¹⁄₁₆in thick

permanent marker pen

ribbon

picture

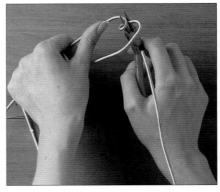

1 Using round-nosed (snub-nosed) pliers, carefully bend the 3mm/⅛ in aluminium wire into a rectangle measuring 15 x 20cm/6 x 8in. At the fourth corner, twist the wire into a heart shape. Do not cut off the wire.

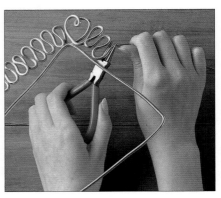

2 Bend the wire into a series of filigree loops to fit along each side of the frame. Form a heart at each corner as you reach it.

3 Leave 1.5cm/½ in of excess wire spare at the last corner and cut off.

4 Cut a 15 x 40cm/6 x 16in rectangle of small-gauge chicken wire and fold it in half. Bend the filigree out of the way and use 1mm/½₅in aluminium wire to bind the chicken wire to the inner rectangle.

5 Bend the filigree back into place and bind it on to the inner rectangle.

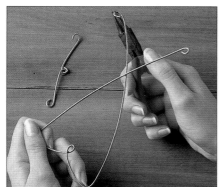

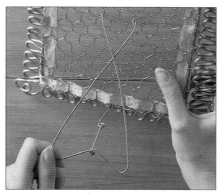

6 To make a support for the frame, cut a 48cm/19in length of galvanized wire. Mark the wire at intervals of 18cm/ 7in, 6cm/2½ in, 6cm/2½ in, and 18cm/ 7in. Bend the wire into a crossed-triangle, forming a loop in the centre and at each end. Cut two short pieces of wire and make a loop at each end. Link the two pieces together and close the loop firmly.

7 Thread the ribbon around the edges of the chicken wire, looping it around each corner so that it lies flat. Attach the support to the frame by opening the loops slightly and then closing them around the chicken wire near the top. Attach one end of the two short linked pieces to the loop in the bottom of the support, and the other end to the base of the frame.

8 Position your picture on the frame and secure it by threading a ribbon through the wire from the back, and looping it around the corners.

This attractive frame incorporates two metal foils, one copper and one brass. The brass pins used to attach the foil to the frame also form a decorative accent in this otherwise simple design.

Metal Foil Frame

you will need
protective gloves
copper foil
scissors or wire cutters
wide, flat wooden frame
dry ballpoint pen
metal ruler
craft knife
self-healing cutting mat
tack hammer
brass escutcheon pins
bradawl (awl)
brass foil
wire (steel) wool
black felt
scissors
fabric glue and brush

1 Cut pieces of copper foil to fit over the frame, allowing for overlaps around the inner rebate and outer edge. Place the frame face down on the foil. Score the foil with a dry ballpoint pen around the inner rebate and outer edge. Remove the frame. Using a metal ruler and craft knife, cut out the corners on the outer edge in line with the score marks. Cut the inner rebate window and mitre the corners.

2 Fold the inner rebate foil around the moulding. Tack it on to the frame with small brass pins – you will need to make the pin holes with a bradawl (awl). Repeat on the outer edge.

3 Hammer the brass foil in place in the same way. Hammer pins at the edges of the brass foil.

4 Using wire (steel) wool, score the copper foil in small circular motions.

5 Cut a piece of black felt to cover the back of the frame. Cut out the window. Stick in place with fabric glue.

Stylized painting on tinware is part of the popular art of India and Latin America. Fine-gauge tin is stamped with decorative patterns and high-lighted with translucent paints. This mirror frame follows the tradition.

Painted Tinware Mirror

you will need

sheet of tin plate, 30 gauge (0.3mm/¹⁄₈₃in thick)

marker pen

ruler

work shirt and protective leather gloves

tin snips (shears)

90° and 45° wooden blocks

bench vice

hide hammer

file

graph paper

scissors

saucer

pencil

square mirror tile

masking tape

sheet of chipboard

panel pins (brads)

tack hammer

centre punch

ball hammer

chinagraph pencil

soft cloth

translucent paints

paintbrush

aluminium foil, 36 gauge (0.1mm/¹⁄₂₅₀in thick)

epoxy resin glue

copper foil, 40 gauge (0.08mm/¹⁄₃₀₀in thick)

D-ring hanger

1 For the frame, draw a 30cm/12in square on a sheet of tin. Draw a 1cm/½in border inside the square. Draw diagonal lines across the corners of the inner square. Wearing protective clothes, cut out the 30cm/12in square with tin snips (shears). Cut along the diagonal lines at the corners.

2 Firmly clamp the 90° block of wood in a bench vice. Place the mirror frame on the wooden block with the ruled edge of the tin resting on the edge of the block. Using a hide hammer, tap along the edge of the tin to turn it over to an angle of 90°.

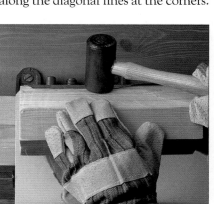

3 Turn the frame over. Hold the 45° block of wood inside the turned edge and hammer the edge over. Remove the block and hammer the edge completely flat. Finish the remaining three edges of the frame in the same way. Carefully file the corners of the mirror frame to remove any sharp edges.

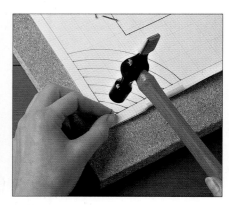

4 Cut a piece of graph paper the same size as the frame. Using a saucer as a template, draw the corner lines on to the paper. Draw in the central square, slightly larger than the mirror tile. Tape the pattern to the back of the frame. Secure the frame to a piece of chipboard with panel pins (brads).

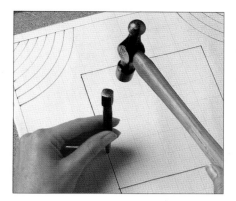

5 Place the point of the centre punch on a drawn line of the inside square and tap it with the ball hammer to make an indentation. Move the punch 3mm/⅛in along the line and tap it to make the next mark. Continue along all the lines.

6 Unpin the frame from the board and remove the pattern. Using a chinagraph pencil, draw a square halfway along each edge between the corner decorations. Draw a heart in each square. Pin the frame to the board again and punch an outline around each square and heart.

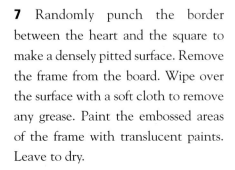

7 Randomly punch the border between the heart and the square to make a densely pitted surface. Remove the frame from the board. Wipe over the surface with a soft cloth to remove any grease. Paint the embossed areas of the frame with translucent paints. Leave to dry.

8 Place the mirror tile on aluminium foil and draw around it. Draw a 1.5cm/⅝in border around the outline. Cut out the foil, snipping the corners at right angles. Glue the tile to the centre of the foil. Glue the edges of the foil over the tile. Cut four small squares of copper foil and glue one square in each corner of the tile.

9 Glue the mirror to the centre of the frame. Glue the hanger to the back of the frame. Allow the glue to dry thoroughly before hanging up the mirror.

This imposing little frame is made from nothing more substantial than cardboard, galvanized wire and some metallic paint, yet it looks weighty and solid, and even has its own wire stand.

Zigzag Wire Frame

you will need

tracing paper

pencil

galvanized wire, 2mm/1/12 in, 3mm/1/8 in and 1mm/1/25 in

tape measure

wire cutters

long-nosed pliers

soldering iron, solder and flux

thick cardboard

craft knife

metal ruler

cutting mat

double-sided adhesive tape

bradawl (awl)

silver metallic paint

paintbrush

epoxy resin glue

1 Trace the template at the back of the book. Cut four lengths of 2mm/1/12in wire each 70cm/28in and, using long-nosed pliers, bend each length to match the spiral zigzag shapes along one side of the frame.

2 Cut ten lengths of 2mm/1/12in wire each 30cm/12in and curl each one into a tight S-shape with the pliers.

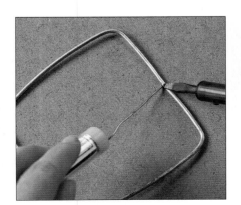

3 Cut a 40cm/16in length of 3mm/1/8 in wire and bend it into a square to form the centre of the picture frame. Arrange the ends in the middle of one side. Solder the ends together.

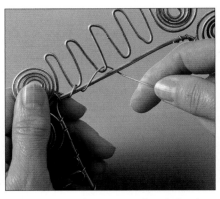

4 Using 1mm/1/25 in wire, bind the four side sections to the central frame.

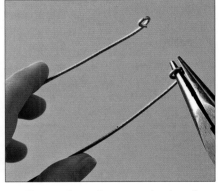

5 To make the stand, bend a 30cm/12in length of 2mm/1/12 in wire into a narrow U-shape, then curl each end into a tight loop.

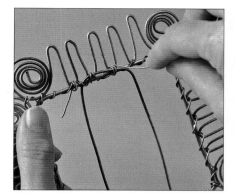

6 Using 1mm/¹⁄₂₅in wire, bind the stand centrally to the back of the top of the frame.

7 Cut two pieces of cardboard to fit the frame, using a craft knife and metal ruler and working on a cutting mat. Cut a window out of the front and a slightly larger window from the back section. Reserve the central part of the back. Stick the frames together using double-sided tape.

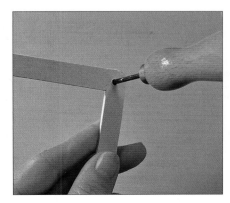

8 Using a bradawl (awl), pierce a small hole in each corner of the picture holder. Paint the front silver.

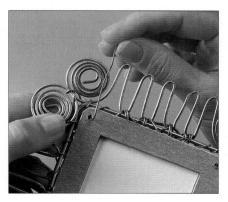

9 Bind the picture holder to the frame at each corner using short lengths of fine wire.

10 Use epoxy resin glue to stick the small S-shapes around the frame. Insert the picture and the cardboard backing board.

Flowers, Beads
and Fabric

Flowers, beads and fabrics can all be used to embellish a plain frame, to add texture, charm and delicacy. You don't need to be a skilled stitcher to use felt, or an expert gardener to utilize dried and silk flowers, but decorative stitching can add another dimension to a frame, and a garden full of flowers gives you greater choice for drying. What is more important, however, is a feel for the decorative potential of these materials.

Any kind of fabric can be used to cover a frame. As only a small amount is needed for a moderate sized frame, you may want to splash out on the most luxurious silks and velvets to enhance a room scheme.

Materials and Equipment

Artificial flowers

Silk flowers of many kinds are available from milliners and craft suppliers. Crepe paper flowers could also be used to decorate frames.

Beads

Use tiny rocaille and bugle beads like glitter, sprinkled on to a glued surface. Stitch or glue larger beads on to frames individually. Small beads can also be threaded on to fine wire to create three-dimensional motifs.

Blotting paper

Used for pressing flowers and petals, to absorb moisture. Place sheets in a heavy book with a weight on top, or insert sheets in a flower press.

Craft knife

Used for reducing the bulk of large flowers for pressing.

Dried flowers

Buy commercially dried flowers from florists or dry your own.

Embroidery hoop

Fabric is placed in the hoop to keep it taut for hand or machine embroidery or beadwork.

Embroidery thread (floss)

Stranded embroidery thread is available in hundreds of shades, as well as metallics. Use all the strands together for bold stitching, or separate them for finer effects.

Felt

Available from craft suppliers in small squares and in a wide range of brilliant colours, felt does not fray and can be stitched or glued.

Flower press

A large number of flowers, leaves and petals can be pressed at the same time in a flower press. Pressure is exerted by tightening a screw at each corner. A heavy book can also be used, but it should not be a precious volume as the flowers will exude moisture.

Fusible bonding web

This is used to bond fabrics together in appliqué work. It is supplied on backing paper, which makes it easy to draw and cut out shapes.

Glue

Use rubber-solution (latex) fabric glue or carpet adhesive for attaching fabric covers to frames. Use PVA (white) glue to paint shapes on which to sprinkle small beads or sequins.

Glue gun

This electrically heated gun melts various types of glue supplied in stick form. It gives an instant bond when working with fabric and dried or artificial flowers.

Hessian (burlap)

This strong woven fabric is used as the backing material for ragwork.

Interfacing

Used to reinforce fabrics. Iron-on interfacing is a non-woven material which can be bonded to the wrong side of the fabric.

Iron

Used to set silk paints and iron on fusible bonding web for appliqué. It can also be used to press flowers between sheets of blotting paper.

Metallic gutta

Used to define designs on silk before painting, to prevent the paints bleeding into one another. It is applied using a special applicator which allows fine details to be defined.

Plastic

For a fun frame treatment, cut plastic flower shapes out of plastic bottles and cartons in bright colours.

Raffia

Use undyed raffia to bind twigs, seedheads and other natural materials to decorate frames.

Ribbon

Satin ribbon can be used to trim frames; stronger ribbons such as petersham or grosgrain can be woven together to cover the whole frame. Small ribbon roses make a pretty decoration for silk-covered frames.

Rug hook

This simple hook on a wooden handle is used to hook strips of rag through hessian (burlap) in ragwork. It is available from craft suppliers.

Scissors

Reserve a pair of sharp scissors exclusively for cutting fabrics, as paper and other materials will quickly blunt their edges. Use large scissors for cutting fabric and small, sharp pointed scissors for embroidery threads.

Sequins

These are available in numerous shapes, sizes and colours, separately or sewn into strings. Stitch or glue them to the frame.

Sewing machine

For joining fabrics and for machine embroidery.

Silk paints

These fabric paints can be used to create delicate washes of colour as well as more vibrant effects. Stretch the silk on a wooden frame to hold it taut. The colours can be set using an iron.

Silk pins

These three-pronged pins are used to secure silk stretched over a frame without ripping the fabric.

Staple gun

Used to attach fabric quickly and easily to a wooden frame.

Twigs and sticks

Collect natural objects from the garden or when out walking. Bundles of willow or hazel sticks of equal size can be bought from craft suppliers or garden centres.

Twine

Jute and sisal twine of various thicknesses make natural looking bindings or hangers for frames, or can be coiled into decorations.

Vanishing fabric marker pen

This dressmaker's aid is useful for marking the right side of fabrics when drawing complex designs, as the marks fade away once the work is completed.

Wadding (batting)

Used to back fabrics when making padded frames.

Fabric, beads, and decorative embroidery stitches add charm to a picture frame. You do not need to be a skilled embroiderer – the techniques outlined on these pages show simple ways to create texture.

Techniques

Beadwork

A few coloured beads or sequins can transform a plain fabric frame. All you need is a needle, a length of thread and some beads.

Attaching single beads

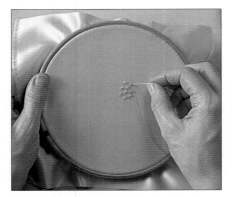

Bring the thread up to the right side and pick up a bead. Sew back through the fabric at the end of the bead.

Attaching bugle beads

Thread a bead and stitch back down at the other end. Hold in place with your thumb while you sew the next bead.

Attaching sequins

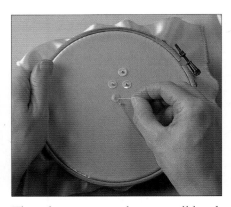

Thread on a sequin then a small bead. Take the needle back through the sequin: the bead will hold the thread.

Painted silk

These steps deal with the preparation of the silk for painting and the setting of the silk dyes afterwards.

Sealing the frame

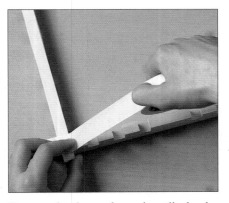

Protect the frame from the silk dye by wrapping it with masking tape before you begin work.

Pinning the silk to the frame

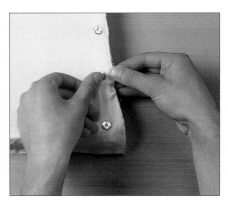

Attach the silk to the frame with silk pins. Pull it taut across the centre first then work out to the corners.

Ironing the finished item

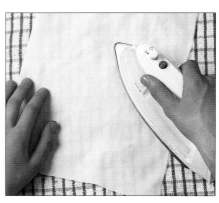

Paint and wash the silk and leave to dry before ironing the fabric on the reverse side to set the colours.

Fusible bonding web

Using fusible bonding web makes cutting out small pieces of fabric much easier. It also helps in appliqué, enabling you to attach the cut-out pieces instantly to the ground fabric.

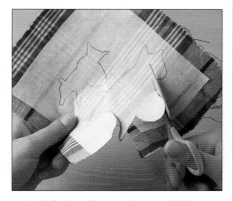

1 Fusible bonding web is useful for stabilizing appliqué pieces, as it fuses on to the fabric when ironed. You can then cut round the shape to be appliquéd, with the interlining in place to act as a stiffener.

2 Fusible bonding web has a backing paper that can be peeled off, leaving a sticky surface. The pieces can then be pressed in place on the ground fabric.

Embroidery

The following stitches are all easy to work, but add subtle decoration to fabric. Experiment using different threads (floss) or work parts of the stitch in a different scale to change the finished appearance.

Machine filigree stitch

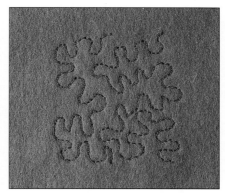

This is a filling stitch particularly effective for quilting, or for cable stitching with gold thread (floss). Use a darning foot on the sewing machine for this stitch, and turn the fabric around and around to achieve the random pattern.

Blanket and buttonhole stitch

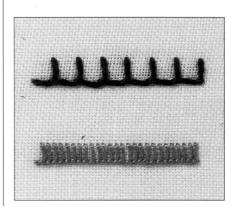

Buttonhole stitch is essentially the same as blanket stitch, except that the stitches are worked closer together. Work buttonhole stitch from left to right. Space the stitches as required, pulling the needle through over the top of the working thread.

Machine satin stitch

This can be worked in free machine embroidery or set for regular stitching. Set the stitch width as desired. Move the embroidery hoop slowly so that the stitches lie close together. Use narrower stitches at the corners so that they taper to a point.

Running stitch

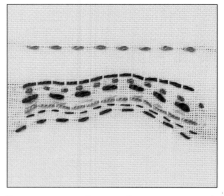

Running stitch can be a tiny prick stitch, a line of basting or a near solid line, depending on the length and spacing of the stitches. Running stitch can be worked as a single line or in multiple rows to fill larger areas. Take the needle in and out across the fabric.

Pressing flowers

Always pick flowers when they are fully open and gather flowers and leaves for pressing on a dry sunny day as any additional moisture in the plant material will lengthen the pressing process.

Preparing

1 Using a craft knife, cut any very bulky flowerheads, such as roses, in half. Then press the flowers.

2 Reduce the height of a thick calyx by snipping close to the petals with small scissors. Be careful not to snip too closely or the petals may fall out.

3 Pare down thick stems using a craft knife. To remove excess moisture from a fleshy stem, place it between the layers of a folded piece of paper towel and squeeze with your fingers.

Pressing

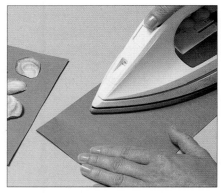

1 The simplest method of pressing flowers is to use a large book. Lay the petals or leaves face down on a folded piece of blotting paper and place between the pages of the book. Put a weight on top, and leave in a warm, dry place for about 6 weeks.

2 To press individual petals, lay them out on a folded piece of blotting paper and press between the pages of a book, as in step 1.

3 A quick method of pressing small flowers, leaves or petals is to iron them. Place them inside a folded piece of blotting paper, and iron using a moderate setting.

Rug hooking   In ragwork, strips of material are hooked through a hessian (burlap) backing cloth. They can be left as a loop pile surface, or sheared with scissors to create a cut pile surface. An effective use of hooking is to combine cut and loop pile within one piece.

1 Place one hand underneath the frame, and loop a strip of fabric between your thumb and forefinger. With your other hand above the frame, push the hook through the hessian (burlap). Feed the fabric loop on to the hook. (The picture shows the underside of the frame.)

2 Pull the hook back up through the hessian, bringing the end of the strip of fabric through to the top.

Backing

Using the finished ragwork as a template, cut out a slightly larger piece of felt. Pin round the edge to attach it in position on the back of the work. Take a needle and matching thread, and slip stitch round the edge, tucking under the excess fabric as you sew.

3 Leave one or two warp threads of hessian to keep the loops close together. Push the hook back through the hessian and feed the fabric loop on to the hook, as before. Pull the hook back up through the hessian to make a loop, approximately 1cm/½in high. Continue. Bring the ends of fabric through to the top, and trim to the same height as the loops.

4 To create a cut pile surface, repeat steps 1–3 but hook the loops to a height of approximately 2cm/¾in. Shear across the top of the loops with a large pair of scissors.

Dried poppy seedheads, twigs and a little paint are all that are needed to decorate these wooden frames. Arrange the materials until you are happy with the designs, then glue them in position.

Poppy Seedhead Frames

you will need

For each frame:

wooden frame, prepared and sanded

multi-purpose glue and brush

brown paper

craft knife

Poppies and Twigs Frame

emulsion (latex) paint

PVA (white) glue

soft cloth

twigs

dried poppy seedheads

Sticks Frame

lichen-covered twigs

multi-purpose glue

Poppies Frame

brown paper tape

dried poppy seedheads

watercolour paint: brown

fine artist's paintbrush

1 To make the Poppies and Twigs Frame (pictured bottom left in the photograph), and the Sticks Frame, (pictured bottom right) glue torn strips of brown paper around the front edges of a wooden frame.

2 For the Poppies and Twigs Frame, dilute the paint and add 5ml/1 tsp glue. Paint a thin colourwash over the frame using the paint and glue mixture. Before it dries, wipe it off with a soft cloth to leave a very thin coat.

3 To decorate the Poppies and Twigs Frame, select twigs and seedheads and cut them to size. Cut through the seedheads with a craft knife.

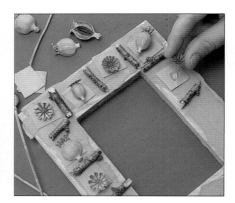

4 Plan your design first, then use glue to stick each piece in position.

5 To make the Sticks Frame, glue lichen-covered twigs around the prepared frame. Leave overnight to dry.

6 To make the Poppies Frame (pictured at the top), cover the back and front of the wooden frame with strips of brown paper tape.

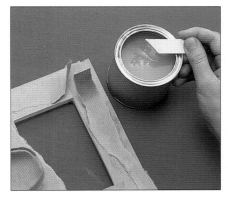

7 Glue rough strips of torn brown paper on to the frame.

8 Add pattern and interest to the brown paper with watercolour paint brushed on in fine cross-hatched lines.

9 Cut off the top of the dried poppy heads with a craft knife and glue them on to the frame.

This frame has a warm, autumnal feel about it, and would make a delightful souvenir of a woodland walk. When collecting the leaves, look for those with unusual colours and shapes.

Pressed-leaf Frame

you will need

selection of leaves in various colours
paper towels
flower press or heavy book
PVA (white) glue and brush
wooden frame, prepared and sanded
acrylic varnish and brush
acrylic crackle glaze
oil paint: raw umber
soft cloth

1 To press leaves, place between layers of paper towels between the pages of a heavy book. Leave for a week.

2 Glue the leaves on to the frame, coating them one at a time with a thin layer of glue and waiting for it to get tacky before sticking the leaf down. Begin by arranging a row of overlapping leaves around the outer edge of the frame. Make a second round, using a different leaf. Select four larger leaves for the corners. Fill in any gaps.

3 Paint a thin layer of varnish over the whole surface and allow to dry. Paint the frame with crackle glaze, following the manufacturer's instructions. Rub a small amount of raw umber oil paint into the cracks in the glaze with a soft cloth, to emphasize the antique effect.

Create an exuberant frame by gluing silk flowers all round it. You can aim for a fairly restrained effect by using just two colours, or restrict your choice of flower to one variety in several colours.

Artificial Flower Mirror Frame

🌸

you will need

frame with mirror

masking tape

scissors

acrylic paint: green

paintbrush

selection of artificial flowers

glue gun and glue sticks

1 Mask the edges of the mirror with tape. Paint the frame with two coats of green acrylic paint. Leave to dry.

2 Cut the stalks off the artificial flowers and arrange them on the frame until you are happy with the design.

3 Glue the flowers in position all around the frame until it is covered. Leave to dry.

This frame shows how ordinary material can be used decoratively. Sisal string is glued into loops and spirals, allowed to dry, then stuck in place. Leave the string in its natural state or finish it with a coat of paint.

String Spirals Frame

❀ ❀

you will need

paper

pencil

pair of compasses

scissors

corrugated cardboard

pen

PVA (white) glue and brush

sisal string

craft knife

emulsion (latex) paint: matt white

paintbrush

1 Draw 5cm/2in diameter circles on paper using a pair of compasses and cut out to use as templates. Draw around the circles on the corrugated cardboard to make a frame shape.

2 Starting in the middle of the circles and working outwards, glue on sisal string in spirals. Fill in each of the circles in this way.

3 At the corners of the frame, fill in the spaces with smaller spirals of string.

4 When the glue is completely dry, cut around the edge of the frame with a craft knife.

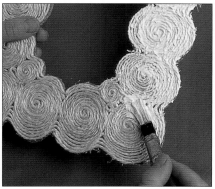

5 Tidy the cut edges of the corrugated cardboard by gluing two lengths of sisal string over them.

6 Paint the front of the frame with matt white emulsion (latex) paint.

7 Make a cardboard back and stand for the frame. Paint them white and allow to dry. Glue the stand in place.

These sparkly picture frames are easy to make. Treat small coloured rocaille and bugle beads like glitter and simply pour them generously on to the glued surface of the frames.

Bead-encrusted Frames

you will need

wooden frames, prepared and sanded

emulsion (latex) or acrylic paint

paintbrushes

palette or plate

PVA (white) glue and brush

small glass rocaille beads in a variety of colours

large sheet of paper

glitter

bugle beads in a variety of colours

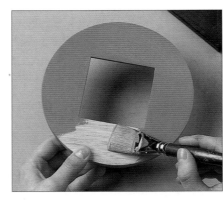

1 Paint each frame in a flat colour and allow to dry. Add another coat if necessary to ensure the bare wood is completely covered.

2 Paint a heart in one corner of a square frame, using glue. Sprinkle rocaille beads over the glue. After the beads have settled for a minute, lightly tap the frame to remove loose ones. Repeat with different colour beads on each corner. Leave to dry.

3 Paint the rest of the frame with glue. With the frame on a large sheet of paper, sprinkle on the glitter. Tap off the excess.

4 Decorate a round frame using bugle beads in various shades of the same colour. Apply glue around the centre of the frame and sprinkle on the beads.

5 Gradually work out to the edge of the frame, applying darker or lighter beads to produce a shaded effect.

This delicate frame encrusted with sequins and beads has a nostalgic character that would suit a special family photograph. Some skill or practice with a needle is required for this project.

Sequins and Beads

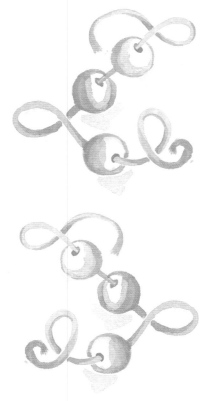

✿✿✿

you will need

pencil

metal ruler

mount (mat) board

cutting mat

craft knife

white calico

scissors

needle

matching sewing thread

satin-backed velvet ribbon, 6cm/2½in wide

green ribbon, 8mm/⅜in wide

small gold glass beads

translucent sequins

clear crystals

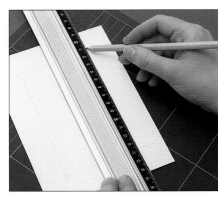

1 Draw the shape of the frame on to a mount (mat) board. The frame should be 4cm/1½ in wide. Working on a cutting mat, cut out the frame, using a metal ruler and craft knife.

2 Cover the back and front of the frame with white calico, oversewing the edges and turning under the raw edges as you go.

3 Measure around the four sides of the frame and cut a piece of satin-backed ribbon slightly longer than this measurement. Fold the ribbon so it is the same width as the sides of the frame, and baste down the satin edge.

4 Using the covered frame as a guide, fold and mitre the corners of the ribbon, tucking under the raw ends.

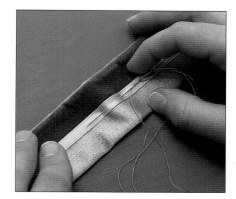

5 Neatly stitch the narrow green ribbon over the seam, using a matching thread colour.

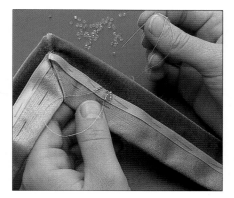

6 Thread four or five small gold glass beads on to a needle and stitch down vertically over the green ribbon. Keeping the beading dense, continue to stitch the beads in place so that the green ribbon is barely visible. Neatly stitch the ribbon frame to the calico-covered frame.

7 Stitch a random selection of translucent sequins and glass beads over the outside edge of the frame.

8 Sew random clear crystals and small glass beads on to the inside edge of the frame.

9 Stitch ribbon to the back of the frame to hold a picture. Leave the top edge unstitched.

Threaded on fine wire, small beads can be turned into enchanting flowers to decorate a plain frame. The colours of the translucent glass beads mimic the delicate hues found in real flower petals.

Flowered Frame

❀ ❀ ❀

you will need

tape measure

wire cutters

beading wire, 0.4mm and 0.2mm

round-nosed (snub-nosed) jewellery pliers

small glass beads: pink, yellow and white

floss thread

wooden frame, prepared and sanded

drill and small drill bit

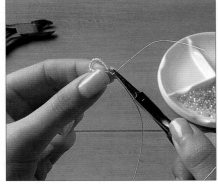

1 To make the leaves, cut 22cm/8¾in of 0.4mm wire. Bend a small hook in one end with pliers to stop the beads falling off. Mix up a few pink beads with the yellow. Bend the wire in half to find the centre point. Thread on 18 beads, push up to the centre point, then bend the wire over to form a beaded loop. Twist the working wire around the stem to secure the beads.

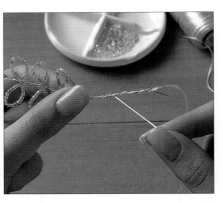

2 Thread on 18 more beads and make another loop. Wrap the working wire around the stem another time and make another loop at the same level. Make two more pairs of loops along the length of the stem. Twist the wire around the stem to secure the beads. Cover the twisted stem by wrapping it with floss thread.

3 Cut 40cm/16in of wire to make a small flower, and 50cm/20in for a large flower. Measure 10cm/4in from one end. Wind the next length of wire twice around your finger to form a loop. The loop is the frame for the beaded flower. Twist the wire to secure the loop.

4 On the next length of wire, pick up 24 pink and white beads for a small flower and 30 for a large one. Push the beads up to the loop framework. Bend the beaded wire back down to the loop frame and twist to secure it.

5 To form the second half of the first petal, thread on some more beads. Twist the wire around the top of the petal and at a right angle to it. Secure the beads on the petal in the same way.

6 Twist the wire around the frame. Make four more petals positioned evenly around the frame.

7 To make the flower centre, thread on 12 yellow beads and twist the wire into a half spiral. Push the working wire through the loop frame and twist it around the stem. The flower centre will stand proud of the frame, and the frame should be covered in beads.

8 Place the flowers and leaves around the frame. When you are happy with the arrangement, mark their positions and drill holes in the frame.

9 Push the wire stems of the beaded flowers and leaves through the holes in the frame and twist them into a knot on the wrong side of the frame.

10 Trim the wire ends. Using the thinner wire, secure the knots on the wrong side of the frame.

A lightweight silk is best for this project, which uses salt to create a soft, watery effect. The silk needs to be damp for the salt grains to take effect, so alternate between painting and adding salt.

Padded Silk Picture Frame

you will need

silk pins

lightweight, plain-weave silk, pre-washed

wooden silk-painting frame

iron-fix (set) silk paints

fine artist's paintbrushes

teaspoon

fine table salt

ruler

pencil

graph paper

craft knife

cutting mat

PVA (white) glue and glue brush

mount (mat) board

25cm/10in square wadding (batting)

dressmaker's scissors

adhesive tape

dressmaker's pins

needle

matching sewing thread

ribbon rose decorations, optional

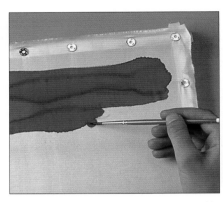

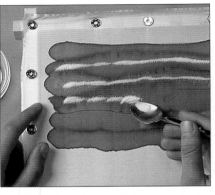

1 Pin a piece of lightweight silk, at least 30cm/12in square, to a silk-painting frame. Using iron-fix (set) silk paints, paint a few stripes of alternate colours on the silk, making the stripes at least 2.5cm/1in wide.

2 While the silk is still damp with the dye, spoon lines of salt grains along the stripes. Continue alternating painting and adding lines of salt grains until the whole surface is covered. Leave the silk to dry. Brush off the salt and iron-fix (set) the dyes according to the manufacturer's instructions.

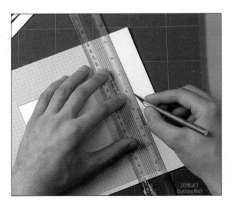

3 Draw a 20cm/8in square on graph paper and cut out. Draw a 10cm/4in square centrally in it and cut it out. Glue the template to the mount (mat) board and cut out the shape.

4 Centre the frame over a square of wadding (batting). Trim off the corners, then fold and stick the surplus wadding down with adhesive tape. Cut a cross in the centre of the wadding, trim it to 2cm/¾in. Clip into the corners, then fold it to the back of the frame and stick it down.

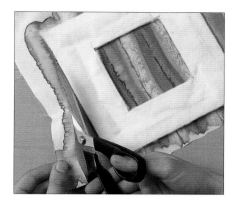

5 Pin the silk to the padded frame, with the wrong side of the silk against the wadding. Trim the excess silk around the frame to 3cm/1¼in. Then cut a cross in the silk inside the frame and trim to 3cm/1¼in all round.

6 Wrap the silk edges over the frame and lace them together with long stitches. Do not pull the silk too tightly and distort the shape.

7 Mitre the corners, fold the flaps over and stitch in place at the back. Sew a small ribbon rose to each inside corner of the frame, if desired.

8 Cut a 20cm/8in square of mount board to make the backing for the frame. Cut a tall, right-angled triangle from the mount board, score along the longest side 1cm/½in from the edge and bend it over to make a stand. Trim the bottom edge and check the board will stand properly.

9 Glue the stand to the backing, starting from the bottom edge. Attach the backing to the frame by gluing along three sides, leaving one side free so that a picture can be slipped inside.

Ribbons are a quick method of adding instant style to a plain picture frame. This design is easy to apply: the ribbons are just woven together at the corners and stapled in place.

Ribbonwork Frame

you will need

medium density fibreboard (MDF),
330 x 250 x 2mm/13 x 10 x ⅛in

pencil

metal ruler

drill and protective face mask

craft knife

wood strip, 106 x 2.5 x 1.25cm/
42 x 1 x ½in

saw

sandpaper (glasspaper)

wood glue and glue spreader

staple gun

hammer

primer: white

paintbrush

navy and white striped ribbon,
5.5m x 15mm/6yd x ⅝in

scissors

1 To mark out the window area of the frame on the medium density fibreboard (MDF), draw a border 4.75cm/1⅞in from the edges. Drill a small hole at each corner in the window area of the frame, then cut out the window between the holes using a metal ruler and craft knife. Wear a protective face mask when working with MDF. Make several shallow cuts rather than one deep one.

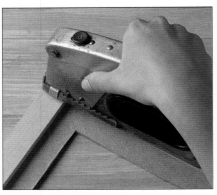

2 Saw the wood strip into two pieces, 33cm/13in long and two pieces 20cm/8in long. Sand the ends and glue them on top of the frame, aligning raw edges. This wood forms the rebate. Staple each joint. Turn the frame over to the right side and staple the MDF to the wood. Hammer the staples flush. Sand any rough edges and apply two coats of white primer. Allow to dry.

3 Cut the ribbon into six 38cm/15in lengths and six 30cm/12in lengths. Spread glue over the front of the frame. Arrange the ribbons on the frame and weave the corners.

4 Lift the frame on to its side. Fold the ribbon ends over the edge and staple down. Once one end of each ribbon is stapled, pull the other end tightly before stapling. Trim the ribbon ends.

5 Glue the remaining ribbon around the edge of the frame with the join at the base. Staple a small piece of ribbon over the join to conceal it.

Felt is easy to use because it has plenty of body and does not fray. Combine two or three different-coloured felts to make a mirror frame in a fun flowery design to hang on the wall.

Fun Felt Frame

you will need

iron

fusible bonding web

felt squares, one each in orange and
lime, and two in lilac

felt-tipped pen

sharp scissors

small circular mirror

craft knife

needle

matching embroidery threads (floss)

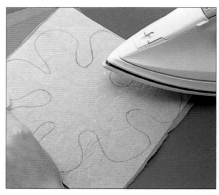

1 Iron the fusible bonding web to the orange, lime and one lilac felt square. On the lilac piece draw a flower outline on the backing paper using the template provided. Draw smaller flowers on the orange and lime squares.

2 Cut out the three felt flower shapes with sharp scissors. Remove the backing paper from the lilac flower and bond it to the other lilac square. Cut around the outline to make a double layer flower.

3 Peel the backing paper off the lime flower and centre it on the lilac one. Fuse the lime flower in place. On the back of the orange flower draw a small circle in the centre, slightly smaller than the mirror, and cut it out.

4 Using a craft knife, make a small cut across the centre of the lime green felt flower, through all three layers of felt. Fuse the orange flower on top of the lime flower.

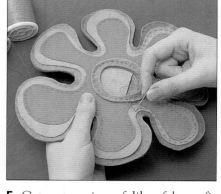

5 Cut out a ring of lilac felt to fit around the circle in the orange flower. Stitch it in place through all the layers using running stitch and a contrasting colour thread (floss). Work running stitches around the edge of the flowers in the same way. Insert the mirror through the slit in the back of the frame. Make a small buttonhole stitch loop to hang the frame.

We are surrounded by brightly coloured plastic containers, and they are a wonderful source of creative material. Make use of some recycled plastic to make this unusual and colourful mirror frame.

Plastic Fantastic

you will need

plastic laundry basket

junior hacksaw

pair of compasses

craft knife

several plastic bottles, lids and caps

pencil

scissors

glue gun

circular mirror

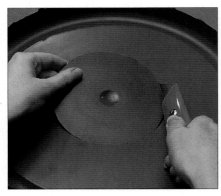

1 Cut off the base of a laundry basket using a junior hacksaw. With a pair of compasses, draw a circle in the middle of the base and cut it out.

2 Select a plastic lid and cut around the rim to make the inner frame for the mirror. Cut down the sides of the bottles and open out into flat sheets.

3 Draw flowers and leaves on to the plastic, using the templates provided, and cut out the shapes, using a pair of sharp scissors.

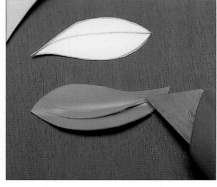

4 Use the craft knife to cut two lines down the middle of each leaf, and lift up the section to make a ridge. Glue the plastic shapes to the frame, using a glue gun. Glue the mirror in place.

5 Glue a bottle cap to the back of the frame, using the glue gun. You can slip the cap over a screw in the wall to hang up the frame.

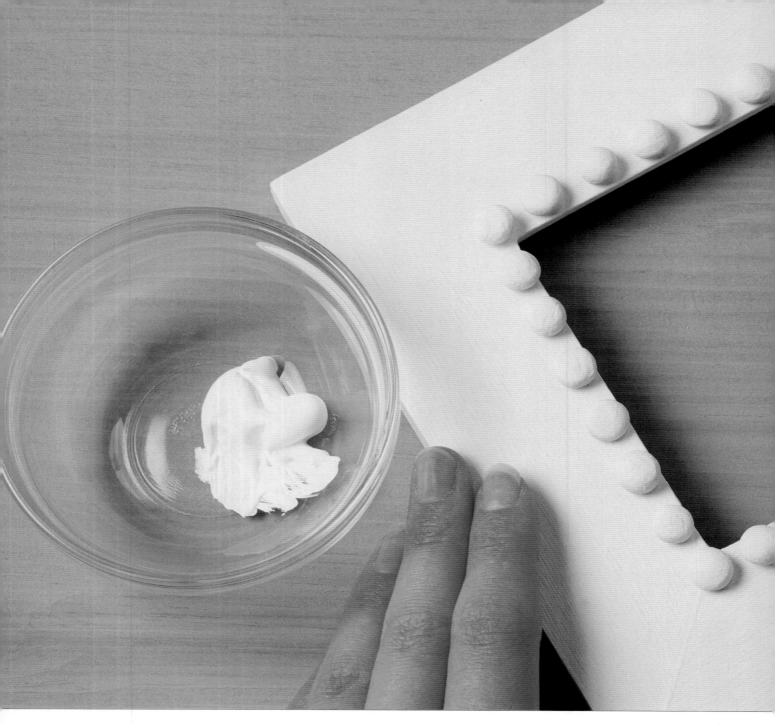

Plaster, Clay
and Mosaic

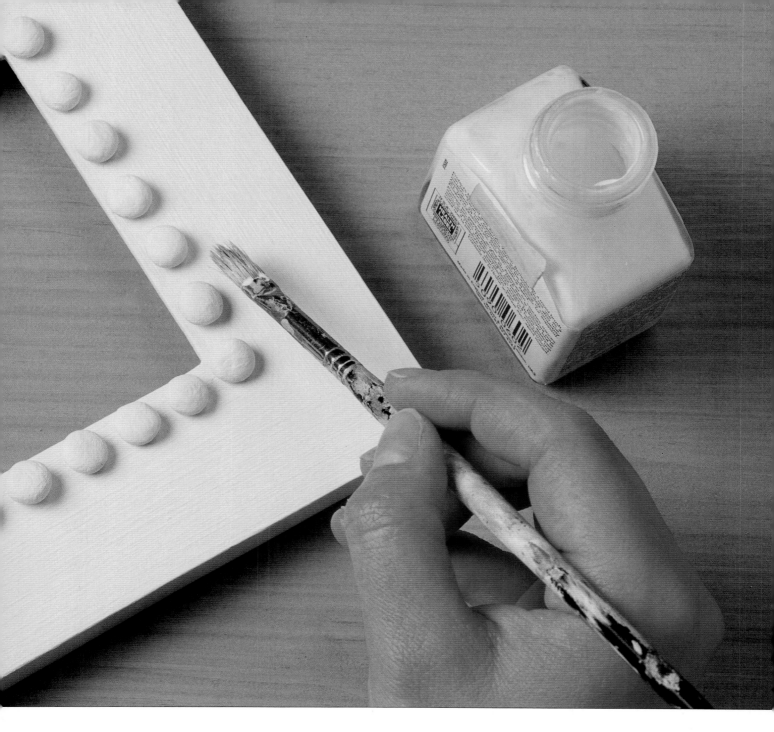

Working with clay and mosaic can be more challenging than working with other media, but the end results can be stunning. You can mould decorative motifs to glue on to a plain frame, or model the whole frame from clay. Choose from the wide variety of colours available or tint the clay yourself. Use mosaic tiles, smashed china, gemstones or mirror tiles to create a range of original and individual mosaic frames.

Plaster is rather fragile for a frame, unless it is very thick, but it can be moulded into lovely decorations for wooden frames. Modelling clay is more durable, and can be strengthened by baking or adding hardeners.

Plaster and Clay Materials

Modelling clay
There are many brands and qualities. Air-dried clay does not require firing.

Plaster
Modelling plaster is always added to the water to mix. Measure the amount of water needed by pouring it into the mould, sprinkle in dry plaster until it starts to mound up out of the water, then stir it in.

Polymer clay
This modelling plastic is available in many colours and special finishes such as fluorescent and metallic. It is hardened by baking at a low temperature in a domestic oven.

Shells
Embed small seashells in a clay frame or incorporate in mosaic.

Talcum powder
Sprinkle on boards and cutters to stop them sticking to the clay.

Wire
Embed a wire hook in the back of a clay frame while it is still soft.

Wood
Cut bases for plaster or clay frames from plywood or medium density fibreboard (MDF), or use planks from wooden fruit crates.

Acrylic varnish
Used for protecting painted clay and plaster surfaces.

Glass nuggets and stones
Embed decorative stones and beads in clay frames. Use glass nuggets if they are to be baked with polymer clay.

Glue
PVA (white) glue can be used as a sealant. Two-part epoxy resin glue is very strong and can be used to join hardened polymer clay and to attach hanging fixtures.

Metal leaf
Use Dutch metal imitation gold or silver leaf or apply copper or aluminium leaf to clay or plaster for decoration.

Mirror tiles
These can be inserted into frames to make small mirrors, or broken and embedded in clay. Wear gloves and safety goggles when breaking glass.

Moulds and modelling tools for plaster and clay work are available in many different shapes, but you can find much of what you need in the kitchen, and ordinary utensils may give you fresh ideas for designs.

Plaster and Clay Equipment

Modelling tools

A range of different shapes and sizes is useful for working with modelling and polymer clay.

Moulds

Specialist moulds are available for plaster, but you can also use containers such as baking tins or ice-cube trays.

Nail file or emery board

Used for filing hardened clay smooth before painting or sealing.

Nylon scouring pad

Used for smoothing rough plaster.

Petroleum jelly

For greasing plaster moulds to allow the hardened plaster to be removed.

Rolling guides

Place two strips of wood of equal depth on each side of a piece of clay and use as guides to roll the clay evenly.

Rolling pin and board

Use a domestic rolling pin for large pieces of clay and a small, cake decorator's rolling pin and non-stick board for small pieces.

Tissue blade

Designed for taking human tissue samples, this very sharp blade is used to cut thin slices from polymer clay.

Brayer

A small roller, like a printing ink roller, can be used to roll out very small pieces of clay, to smooth a clay surface or to rub over metal leaf to help it adhere.

Cocktail sticks (toothpicks)

Used to make very small holes in clay.

Drinking straws

The end of a plastic drinking straw can be used to cut out tiny circles in clay.

Found objects

Many different objects can be used to impress designs in soft clay.

Greaseproof (waxed) paper

Assemble polymer clay frames on greaseproof paper so that they can be moved to the oven for hardening.

Knives

Use a sharp kitchen knife or a craft knife to trim clay. Use a round-bladed knife to indent clay.

Glass tesserae (the individual pieces of the mosaic) can be bought from specialist suppliers in many colours, but imaginative mosaics can also be created using broken tiles and pieces of second-hand china.

Mosaic Materials and Equipment

Adhesives

PVA (white) glue is often used to stick tesserae to a wooden base when the mosaic is for indoor use.

Ceramic tiles

Break glazed tiles into small irregular chunks for mosaic work. Wrap in sacking and hit with a hammer, then shape the pieces with tile nippers.

Crockery

Old plates and cups make very interesting tesserae, as they are often decorated with patterns.

Glass tiles

Square mosaic tiles in opaque glass are manufactured with one flat and one corrugated side.

Notched spreader

Used for spreading tile cement when creating mosaics.

Tile cement and grouting

Available in a range of colours, for applying mosaic tiles and grouting the finished work. Tile cement can be coloured with paint.

Tile nippers

Used for cutting glass tiles to size for the edges of designs and for shaping broken china for mosaic.

Clay is a wonderfully versatile material, which can be used to produce many different effects. Instructions are given here for the basic techniques that have been applied to many of the projects in this book.

Techniques

Working with polymer clay

Make sure your hands are scrupulously clean before working with polymer clay as it will pick up any dirt and dust around. Also wash your hands when changing from one colour to another to avoid colour contamination.

Mixing colours

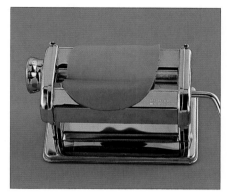

A pasta-making machine is excellent for mixing colours. Feed two differently coloured sheets through the machine together, feeding them from opposite sides. As they go through the machine they will become fused and any air bubbles will be squeezed out.

Metallic finishes

1 Lay a sheet of transfer leaf over the clay. As you do so, roll over it using a brayer to eliminate air bubbles. Rub all over the backing tissue before gently and slowly peeling it off.

Rolling out

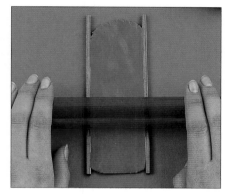

Roll the clay out on a smooth, clean surface, using a smooth rolling pin. To ensure an even thickness, roll the clay between two pieces of metal, wood or plastic of the depth you require. If the clay is sticky, dust it with a thin film of flour or talcum powder.

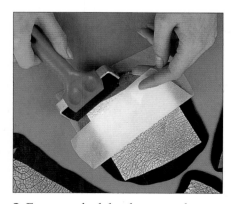

2 For a cracked finish, cover the surface of the applied metal leaf with paper and run the roller over it. The cracking on silver and gold is finer than on copper or aluminium.

Working with modelling clay

Modelling clay can be sticky to work with. A light dusting of talcum powder on the work surface and on the rolling pin helps prevent the clay from sticking and distorting your designs.

Rolling out

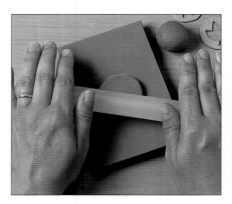

1 Work on a surface that can easily be wiped clean. Take enough clay to complete the section you are working on. Flatten the clay with your hands then roll with the pin. Turn the clay around and keep rolling until you have a smooth, even slab.

2 A small non-stick rolling board and rolling pin designed for cake decorating are especially useful for rolling out small pieces of clay for delicate work.

Embossing and moulding

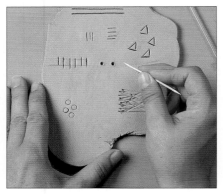

Before starting a project that requires surface decoration, practise on a spare piece of clay. Make small holes with a cocktail stick (toothpick), the rounded end of a knife, or by pressing a drinking straw into the clay and removing it with the plug of clay inside. Scratch the surface of the clay and emboss with found objects.

Cutting around a template

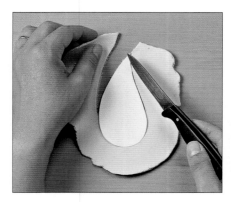

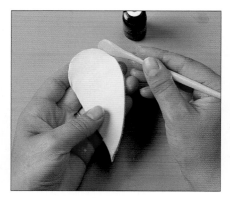

1 Some brands of modelling clay can be quite fibrous when cut, so neaten the edges with a modelling tool or the edge of a knife as you work. Moisten the tool slightly with water as needed.

2 Smooth the edges with a modelling tool for a more rounded edge or use your fingertips, lightly moistened with hand cream.

Filing rough edges

When the work is dry, remove any rough edges with a nail file or emery board. Sand carefully, as dry clay can be powdery and is delicate. Use a nail file for reaching small areas and fine sandpaper for large surfaces. Seal with PVA (white) glue.

Working with mosaic

When embarking on your first mosaic, use a simple design, such as a geometric pattern, and concentrate on finding the right colour combinations. Often, this can produce the most effective mosaics.

1 Hold the material to be cut between the tips of the cutting edges of a pair of tile nippers. Squeeze the handles together, and the tesserae should break in two along the line of impact. Nippers are also useful for cutting tesserae into a specific shape.

2 When breaking up larger ceramics, such as tiles, and if regular shapes are not required, break the material with a hammer. When doing this, always wear a pair of goggles or cover the tile or china with a piece of sacking.

3 Mark the frame into small, equally spaced sections. Using a dark pencil or a marker pen, draw a simple motif in each section. Here, the motif is a daisy.

4 Mix up some cement-based tile adhesive and, working on a small area at a time, spread it along the lines of your drawing. Press the tesserae firmly into the cement. Choose shapes that echo those of the design, for example, the petal shapes of the flower. When each motif is tiled, thoroughly wipe off any excess cement with a sponge and leave to dry overnight.

5 Break up tiles in the background colour with a hammer. Working on a small area of the frame at a time, spread cement-based adhesive on to the unfilled sections and press the tesserae into it. When the surface is covered, use small pieces of the background colour to tile along the outer edges of the frame, ensuring that the tesserae do not overlap the edge. Leave to dry for 24 hours.

6 Mix powdered grout with water. If you wish the grout to have a colour, add cement dye, vinyl matt emulsion or acrylic paint to the mixture (for indoor use, cement dye is not essential). Wearing rubber (latex) gloves, spread the grout over the surface using a squeegee or a flexible knife. Rub the grout into the gaps with your fingers.

Modelling plaster is readily available and easy to use. Look around for unusual cake tins or moulds in which to create plaster shapes. The red frame has been tinted using shoe polish as a quick colouring.

Plaster Cast Frame

you will need

springform ring cake tin (pan)

petroleum jelly

modelling plaster

bowl

jug (pitcher) (optional)

flexible plastic decorative ice cube tray

nylon scouring pad

soft cloth

coloured shoe polish

wooden frame, prepared and sanded

paintbrush

emulsion (latex) paint: white

strong glue

glue brush

1 Grease the inside of the cake tin (pan) with petroleum jelly. Assemble the tin and ensure it is watertight.

2 To make the plaster, add modelling plaster to a bowl of water until a mound of plaster forms out of the water. Mix the plaster with your hand.

3 Pour the plaster into the cake tin mould. You may find it easier to use a jug (pitcher). When the tin is half full, pour the excess plaster into a decorative ice cube tray to make motifs for use on the second frame. Tap the moulds to remove any air bubbles from the bottom and sides.

4 After about 4–5 minutes, the plaster in the tin will begin to harden. Make an indentation around the centre, removing some of the plaster, to make a rebate for the picture.

5 When the plaster is completely hard, remove it from the mould and smooth off the sides and any rough edges with a nylon scouring pad.

6 Allow the plaster to dry thoroughly – this can take up to a week. With a soft cloth, apply a liberal coating of coloured shoe polish to colour and seal the plaster. The plaster will absorb some of the colour.

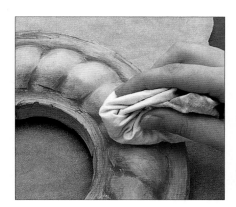

7 After about 10 minutes, rub off the shoe polish with the soft cloth, leaving traces of colour in the recesses.

8 To decorate a wooden frame, turn out the plaster shapes from the ice cube tray and smooth off the edges of the bases with the nylon scouring pad.

9 Paint the frame with white emulsion (latex) paint. When the paint is dry, glue on the plaster shapes. Allow the glue to dry completely.

These pure white frames are co-ordinated yet individually decorated. Restrained, geometric relief designs add interest with the play of light and shadow, yet do not overwhelm the contents of the frames.

Geometric Clay Frames

you will need

3mm/⅛in rolling guides

rolling pin

white modelling clay

small round and square metal cutters (cookie cutters)

cocktail stick (toothpick)

round-ended knife

masking tape

acrylic or emulsion (latex) paint: white

paintbrushes

wooden frames, prepared and sanded

emery board

wood glue

matt acrylic varnish

1 Roll out a small piece of clay to an even thickness of about 3mm/⅛in. Using a round cutter, cut out several shapes from the clay.

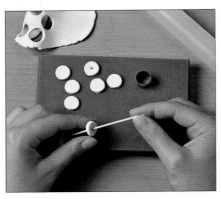

2 Pierce the centre of each clay disc with a cocktail stick (toothpick) and allow to dry.

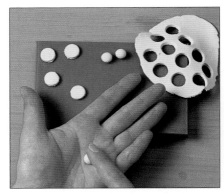

3 For an alternative design, cut out a number of clay discs as before. Roll each disc in the palm of your hand, then between your fingers to make a number of evenly sized balls. Allow the balls to dry thoroughly.

4 Roll out more clay and cut out small squares using a square cutter. Decorate the squares with different marks using the flat end of a knife. Aim to have about five different designs. Stick each to a flat surface with masking tape so that the edges do not curl. Allow to dry completely.

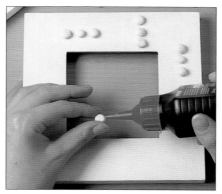

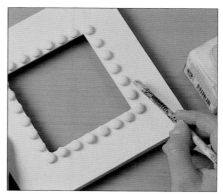

5 Apply several coats of white acrylic or emulsion (latex) paint to the frames, allowing each coat to dry before applying the next.

6 File any rough edges from the clay motifs using an emery board. When you are satisfied with the arrangement stick each in place with wood glue.

7 When the glue is dry, apply one or two coats of white paint to the entire frame, followed by several coats of matt acrylic varnish. Allow each coat to dry before applying the next.

Whether you want to jot down reminders for yourself or to leave important messages for somebody else, this chalkboard in its rustic frame is perfect for the potting shed or to hang on the kitchen wall.

Modelled Flower Garden Frame

you will need
wooden fruit crate
saw
small chalkboard
mitre box
wood glue
staple gun
paintbrush
acrylic paints in a variety of colours
glue gun
modelling clay
modelling tools
rolling pin
sharp knife
tracing paper
pencil
scissors
medium artist's paintbrush

1 Remove the sides of the fruit crate and from it cut four lengths to fit the dimensions of the board. Mitre the corners. Use wood glue, then a staple gun, to hold the joints firmly. Paint the front of the frame green. Allow to dry. Glue the chalkboard to the back of the frame.

2 To model a flower, roll six balls of clay the same size. Put one ball aside until step 3. Squeeze the remaining five into a point at one end. Using a rounded modelling tool, press each into a fat petal. Arrange the petals into a flower shape.

3 Place the last ball in the flower centre and indent with a rounded modelling tool. For the fence, roll out the clay and cut two strips each 1cm/½in wide to fit across the frame. Cut short strips for the posts. Trim the top of each post to a point.

4 For the leaves, roll out the clay, then cut basic leaf shapes and smooth out the edges with your fingers. Use a pointed modelling tool to trace a central vein on each one. Make 12 leaves.

5 Trace the templates provided for the pot and watering can and cut out. Cut out the shapes from clay, using the templates as a guide. Smooth the clay edges with your fingers.

6 For each three-dimensional pot at the bottom of the chalkboard, roll a ball of clay in your hand, then model it into a small pot shape. Let all the clay pieces dry for a few days.

7 Using an artist's paintbrush, paint the shapes with acrylic paints in bright colours, and allow to dry.

8 Use a glue gun to attach the picket fence and the other decorations to the chalkboard frame.

Small decorated mirror frames are always appealing and this one is easy and fun to make. The colourful, bright-eyed lizards would be an ideal decoration for a child's bedroom with an animal theme.

Modelled Lizard Mirror Frame

you will need

1 block light turquoise polymer clay

brayer (small roller)

craft knife

round mirror, 13.5cm/5¼in diameter

½ block fluorescent pink and

¼ block magenta polymer

clay, mixed 2:1

3 blocks dark turquoise polymer clay

small amounts polymer clay: grey,

black and white

smoothing tool

D-ring

epoxy resin glue

1 Roll out the light turquoise clay to about 5mm/¼in thick. Cut five curved strips using the template at the back of the book and place them carefully around the edge of the mirror.

2 From the mixed pink and magenta clay, roll out two long sausage shapes, one slightly thicker than the other. Use the thinner sausage to edge the inner ring of the border, and the thicker sausage to edge the outer ring.

3 Make the lizards from dark turquoise clay. For the legs, roll short sausages, flatten one end and bend for the knee and foot joints. Make 20.

4 For each body, roll a tapered sausage from a piece of dark turquoise clay. Create a neck in the thicker end by rolling between your two index fingers and flatten out the head. Make four more bodies.

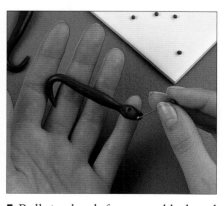

5 Roll tiny beads from grey, black and white clay for the eyes. Position the grey first and flatten, then add the black and finally the white on top. ▶

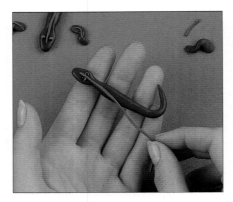

6 Roll thin strands of light turquoise clay to make a stripe for each lizard's back and its legs.

7 Make a thin tapering sausage from the pink clay and slice thinly to make subtly graded discs. Make approximately 18 per lizard. Roll the discs into balls, flatten and apply to either side of the back stripe.

8 Position the legs at equal intervals on the mirror surround so that all the front legs cover up the joins in the border. Press them into position using a smoothing tool.

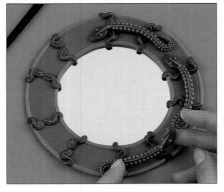

9 Place the lizards' bodies on top of the legs, carefully but firmly enough to ensure that they join properly. Bake for three-quarters of the manufacturer's recommended baking time.

10 Form another, thicker pink sausage and flatten it into a flat circle using the brayer (small roller). Press it in position around the back of the mirror edge, making sure that it adheres well.

11 Roll out a thin sheet of pink clay and make a semi-circle to fit within the back surround. Bake the mirror frame for the remainder of the recommended cooking time.

◀ **12** To position the D-ring for hanging, loop a thin strip of clay through the ring and make an indentation on the semi-circle but do not attach it yet. Remove the strip and the semi-circle and bake separately on a flat surface. When cool, glue the shape to the back of the mirror then add the tab, ensuring that the D-ring can move freely.

This recipe will make eight to ten frames. The colours are built up in blocks, from which you take slices for each frame. To make one frame, cut out all the basic shapes from 2mm/¹⁄₁₆in thick sheets of green clay.

Stitched Clay Frame

you will need

polymer clay: 2 blocks green, large
block black, 2 blocks blue

tissue blade

smooth paper

small roller

craft knife

needle

greaseproof (waxed) paper

embroidery thread (floss): blue
and yellow

corrugated or thick cardboard

knitting needle

jewellery head pins and pliers

epoxy resin glue

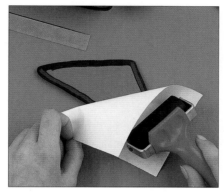

1 To make the roof, mould half a block of green clay into a triangular wedge. Cover with a thin skin of black clay. Then cover two sides with a thick blue layer and one side with black. Surround the whole with a thin layer of black. Using the tissue blade, trim the end of the wedge, then take off a thick slice across the wedge. Place a sheet of smooth paper over this and roll the slice to the required size.

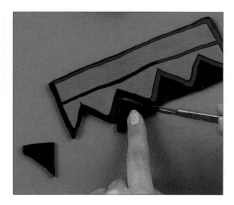

2 Make a long oblong block in green clay, about 16 x 2.5 x 3cm/6½ x 1 x 1¼in. Surround it with a thin skin of black clay. Place a thick blue strip along the bottom. Cover the top with black for two-thirds of the length and with blue for the remainder, and finally with a thin layer of black. Make two smaller oblongs, about 6 x 2 x 3cm/2½ x ¾ x 1¼in, one of black, the other of green. Slice both in half then cut diagonally across each to make triangles.

◀ **4** Insert the black triangles between the green ones and compress the whole assembly, without distorting any of it, to pack all the elements together. Using the tissue blade, take off a thin 3mm/⅛in slice. Place a sheet of smooth paper over this and roll smooth. Cut out the black triangles with a craft knife, leaving a black edging. This will be the base. ▶

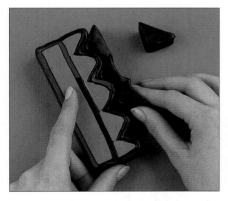

3 Centre three green triangles on the oblong block. Cut the last one in half and place at each end. Wrap the entire structure with thin black clay. Cover one side and halfway along the ridges with a thick blue layer and the remainder with a thick black layer. Add a thin black layer over the blue right down the opposite side.

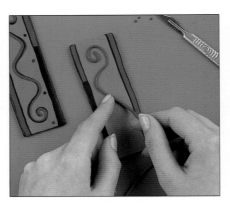

5 Make up another block, like the base block in step 2, but wider, about 16 × 4 × 3cm/6½ × 1½ × 1¼in. Using the tissue blade, take off two thin 3mm/⅛in slices the length of the oblong. Place a sheet of smooth paper over each and roll them smooth. These will be the sides.

6 Decorate the roof and sides. Make an oval cane of blue wrapped in black and cut three slices for the roof. Make long, thin blue and black sausages to make scroll patterns on the roof and sides. Cut tiny discs from the sausages to make spots.

7 Assemble the frame, securing the pieces with small pieces of black clay pressed across the joins at the back. Referring to the finished template for guidance, use a needle to make stitching holes. Add more spots to balance the design if you like. Cover the back with a thin layer of black clay, cutting out the window. Place the frame, face up, on a sheet of greaseproof (waxed) paper and bake following the manufacturer's instructions.

8 Stitch through the prepared holes with thread (floss), referring to the finished illustration. Roll out a 3mm/⅛in thick black rectangle, slightly larger than the window. Place it over a sheet of corrugated cardboard or thick cardboard and press all round it to create a pocket. Pierce a hole near the top using a knitting needle and reinforce it with a ring of clay.

9 Make a small black-wrapped blue cane, press it into an egg shape and cut six slices. Sandwich a jewellery head pin between a pair of slices and kink the wire with pliers. Bake these with the pocket following the manufacturer's instructions.

10 Glue the pocket into position, pressing along the seams to ensure a good join. The gap should be wide enough to slide in a piece of glass and a picture. Glue the jewellery wire shapes in place.

Small mosaic tiles make an attractive Mediterranean-style frame. To keep the project simple, plan the dimensions of the frame to suit the size of the tiles, to avoid having to cut and fit odd-shaped pieces.

Mediterranean Mirror

you will need

pencil

metal ruler

medium density fibreboard (MDF), 18mm/³⁄₄in thick

saw

drill

jigsaw

wood glue

white acrylic primer

paintbrush

tile cement

fine notched spreader

glass mosaic tiles

grout

soft cloth

mirror

narrow frame moulding

2 ring screws

brass picture wire

1 Draw a frame on medium density fibreboard (MDF). Cut it out using a saw. Drill corner holes for the centre and cut this out with a jigsaw. Cut out a shelf and glue to the frame with wood glue. Allow to dry.

2 Prime both sides of the frame and shelf with white acrylic primer to seal it. Allow to dry. Apply tile cement to a small area of the frame, using a fine notched spreader.

3 Apply a random selection of tiles, leaving a 2mm/¹⁄₁₆in gap between each tile. Continue over the rest of the frame, working on a small area at a time. Tile the edges of the frame with a single row of tiles.

4 Allow to dry following the tile cement manufacturer's instructions. Spread grout over the surface of the tiles. Scrape off the excess.

5 Clean off any remaining grout with a soft cloth. Leave to dry thoroughly.

6 Place the mirror glass face down on the back of the frame and secure it with narrow frame moulding, glued in place with wood glue. Allow to dry.

7 Screw two ring screws in place on the back of the mirror, and tie on picture wire to hang the frame.

In this lovely hallway mirror, romantic red hearts and scrolling white lines are beautifully offset by the rich blue background, which sparkles with chunks of randomly placed mirror glass.

Valentine Mirror

you will need

rectangle of plywood, 12mm/½in thick, cut to size required

PVA (white) glue

paintbrush

sharp implement

mirror plate

screwdriver

12mm/½in screws

mirror, cut to size

brown paper

scissors

masking tape

tile cement

soft dark pencil

tile nippers

protective goggles

thin, glazed ceramic household tiles: blue, red and white

rubber (latex) gloves

hammer

heavy protective gloves

mirror tiles

piece of sacking or heavy cloth

notched spreader

dust mask

fine-grade abrasive paper

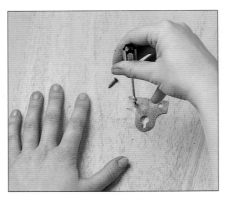

1 Prime both sides of the plywood with diluted PVA (white) glue and leave to dry. Score the front with a sharp implement. Screw the mirror plate to the back of the plywood.

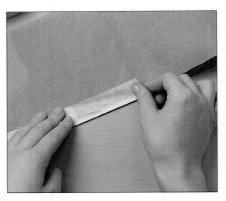

2 Cover the mirror glass with brown paper and tape it in place to protect the glass. Centre the mirror on the plywood and stick it in place using tile cement. Allow to dry.

3 Draw a small heart in the centre of each border and scrolling lines to connect the four hearts. Use the template at the back of the book if desired.

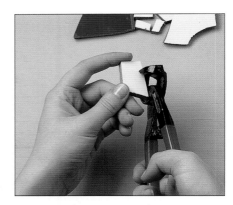

4 Using tile nippers and wearing goggles, cut the blue and red tiles into small, irregular pieces. Cut the white tiles into regular-sized squares.

5 Wearing rubber (latex) gloves, spread the tile cement over the hearts and press in the red tiles. Repeat for the white lines. Scrape off any excess cement and leave to dry.

6 Using a hammer and wearing goggles and gloves, break the blue and mirror tiles. Wrap each tile in a piece of heavy cloth before breaking it.

7 Spread tile cement over the background, then press in the tiles. Leave to dry. Grout the mosaic with cement, wearing rubber gloves as before and using a notched spreader.

8 Wearing a dust mask, carefully sand off any lumps of remaining cement which may have dried on the surface of the mosaic, using fine-grade abrasive paper.

9 For a professional finish, rub tile cement into the back of the plywood board. Remove the protective brown paper from the mirror.

It is hard to believe that this beautiful, shell-encrusted frame started life as a plain wooden one. Texture is built up using neutral-coloured shells, such as limpets and cockles, embedded into tile cement.

Grotto Frame

you will need

assorted shells in neutral colours

wooden frame, prepared and sanded

white tile cement

small palette knife

PVA (white) glue and brush

blue limpet shells

small coloured shells

frosted glass beads

tweezers

small clear glass beads in 3 toning colours

large matchstick

emulsion (latex) paint: white

paintbrush

1 Attach the shells to the frame using white tile cement and a small palette knife. Allow the shells to overlap the edges at the top and sides of the frame to disguise its square shape and to create a grotto-like effect.

2 Continue to cover the frame around the inside edge, allowing the shells to overlap the edge as before.

3 Fill in the gaps between the shells with smaller shells.

4 Select knobbly shells to cover the side and top edges of the frame; attach them with cement as before. Leave to dry for several hours.

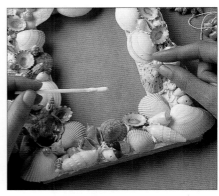

5 Use PVA (white) glue to stick on decorative blue limpets and small coloured shells.

6 To add colour and texture, glue on frosted glass beads, using tweezers to position them.

7 Mix the clear glass beads into some glue. Using a large matchstick, add blobs of this mixture in the gaps between the shells on the frame. Leave the glue to dry.

8 Paint the back of the frame white. If the frame is free-standing, it is important that the back looks attractive, so finish by attaching a few more shells to the top of the frame.

Semi-precious stones, such as agate and carnelian, can be found on some beaches. To identify them, hold them up to the light and they will glow with shades of warm ochre or deep russet.

Rock Pool Mirror

you will need

paper
pencil
metal ruler
scissors
craft knife
cutting mat
polyboard
pair of compasses
bradawl (awl)
wire
PVA (white) glue and brush
circular mirror glass, 10cm/4in diameter
masking tape
small sticks
tile cement
small palette knife or spreader
small pebbles
semi-precious stones
aquarium gravel
watercolour paints
small artist's paintbrush
palette

1 Draw a hexagon template on a piece of paper. Using a craft knife and metal ruler and working on a cutting mat, cut two hexagons from polyboard. Draw a circle 9.5cm/3¾in in diameter in the centre of one of the pieces.

2 Cut out the circle with a craft knife, holding the knife at an angle so that the hole has a sloping edge. Keep the cut-out circle.

3 Using a bradawl (awl), pierce two holes in the hexagon. Thread the wire loop through the holes for hanging the mirror and twist the ends shut.

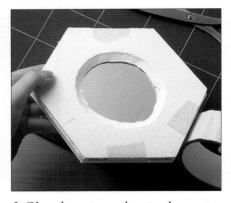

4 Glue the mirror glass in the centre of the backing, with the wire loop on the back. Place the other hexagon right side up on top to form a sandwich, and tape together.

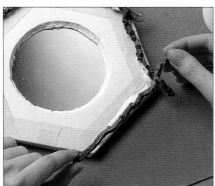

5 Cut sticks to fit along the edges of the frame, overlapping them at the corners. Glue in place. Leave to dry.

6 Replace the cut-out circle to protect the glass. Spread tile cement over the frame, then arrange the pebbles and semi-precious stones on top, lightly pressing them into the cement. Leave the frame to dry.

7 Remove the polyboard circle. Mix the aquarium gravel with PVA (white) glue and fill in the gaps between the stones, especially around the inner edge. Leave to dry. Add a second layer of sticks to the outside edge. Mix watercolour paint with plenty of water and wash over the grout to blend it in.

Templates

Enlarge the templates on a photocopier. Alternatively, trace the design and draw a grid of evenly spaced squares over your tracing. Draw a larger grid on to another piece of paper and copy the outline square by square. Finally, draw over the lines to make sure they are continuous.

Seaside papier mâché mirror, p18

Starry cardboard frame, p17

Swirly mirror, p22–3

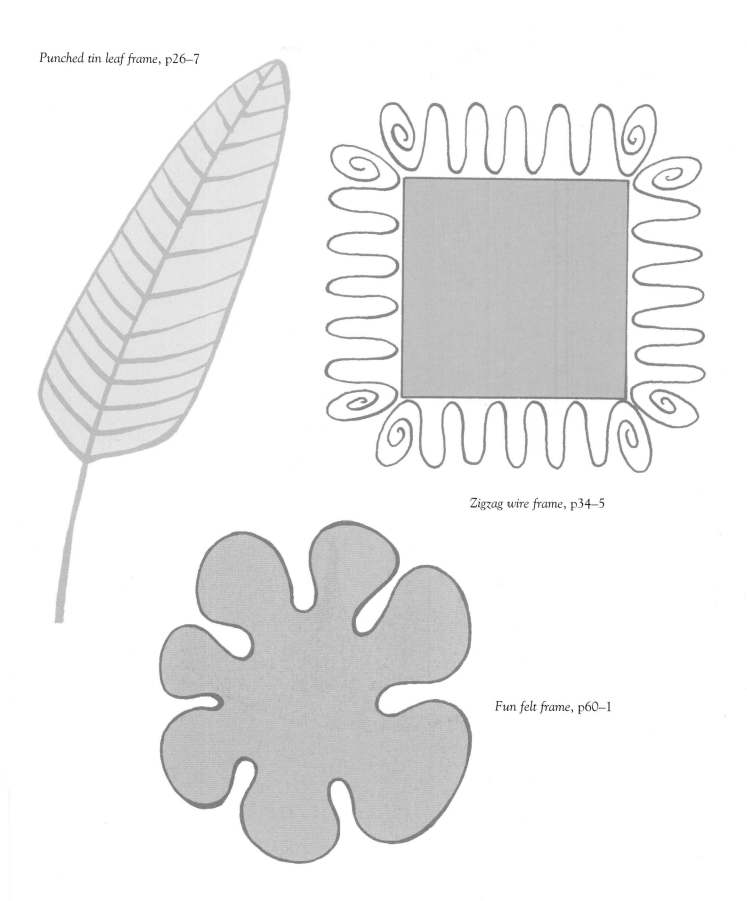

Punched tin leaf frame, p26–7

Zigzag wire frame, p34–5

Fun felt frame, p60–1

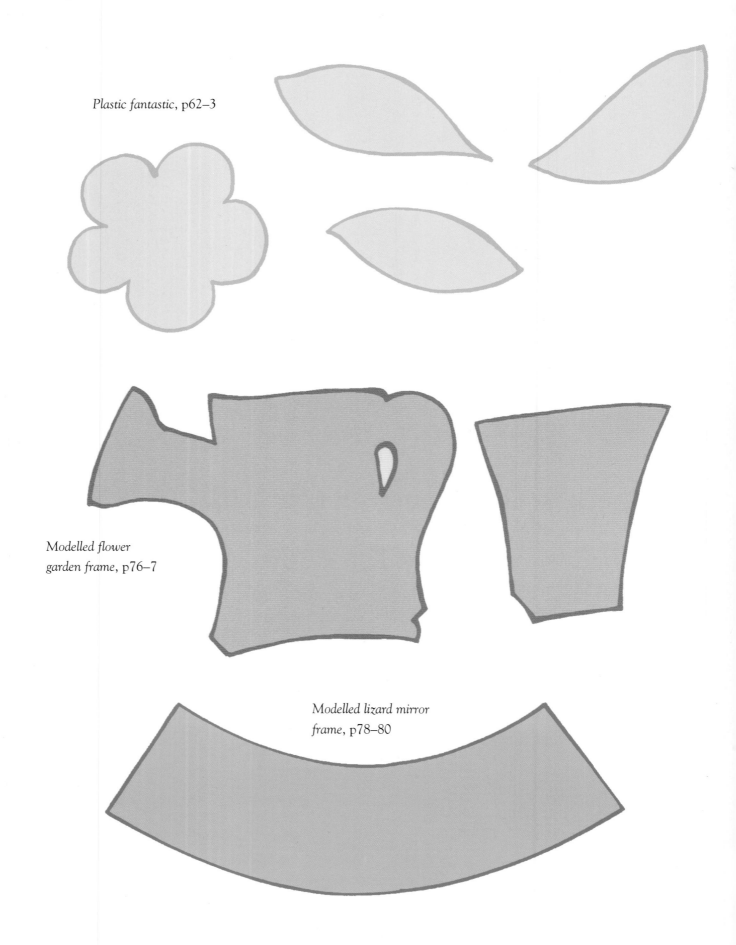

Plastic fantastic, p62–3

*Modelled flower
garden frame, p76–7*

*Modelled lizard mirror
frame, p78–80*

Stitched clay frame, p81–3

Valentine mirror, p86–7

Acknowledgements

The publisher would like to thank the following people for designing projects in this book:

Helen Baird for the Valentine Mirror pp86–7
Petra Boase for the Bead-encrusted Frames pp50–1.
Penny Boylan for the Geometric Picture Frames pp74–5.
Victoria Brown for the Poppy Seedhead Frames pp44–5, String Spirals Frame pp48–9, Fun Felt Frame pp60–1, Plastic Fantastic pp62–3, Plaster Cast Frame pp72–3, Meditteranean Mirror pp84–5.
Sandy Bryant for the Ivy Leaf Frame pp24–5.
Elizabeth Couzins-Scott for the Hammered Paper Frame p19.
Ann Dyson for the Modelled Lizard Mirror Frame pp78–80.

Marion Elliot for the Starry Cardboard Frame p17, Seaside Papier Mâché Mirror p18, Painted Tinware Mirror pp32–3.
Lucinda Ganderton for the Padded Silk Picture Frame pp56–7.
Sandra Hadfield for the Swirly Mirror pp22–3.
Alison Jenkins for the Zigzag Wire Frame pp34–5, Modelled Flower Garden Frame pp76–7.
Rian Kanduth for the Metal Foil Frame pp30–1.
Mary Maguire for the Wire Picture Frame pp28–9, Stitched Clay Frame pp81–3, Grotto Frame pp88–9, Rock Pool Mirror pp90–1.
Michael Savage for the Punched Tin Leaf Frame pp26–7.
Andrea Spencer for the Corrugated Picture Frame p16.
Karen Spurgin for the Sequins and Beads pp52–3.

Isabel Stanley for the Flowered Frame pp54–5.
Dorothy Wood for the Oranges and Lemons Decoupage pp20–1, Ribbonwork Frame pp58–9.

Thanks to the following for individual projects: Ofer Acoo, Deborah Alexander, Michael Ball, Amanda Blunden, Esther Burt, Gill Clement, Louise Gardam, Jill and David Hancock, Rachel Howard Marshall, Terry Moore, Jack Moxley, Oliver Moxley, Deborah Schneebeli-Morrell, Debbie Siniska, Karen Triffitt and Josephine Whitfield.

Thanks to the following photographers: Steve Dalton, Nicki Dowey, Rodney Forte, Michelle Garrett, Rose Jones, Debbie Patterson, Spike Powell, Graham Rae, Steve Tanner, Adrian Taylor, Lucy Tizard, Peter Williams and Polly Wreford.

Index

aluminium foil, embossing, 15

beadwork, 38, 40, 50–5
bonding web, fusible, 38, 41
brass foil, 30–1
brayers, 67

cardboard, 10, 17
chalkboards, framed, 76–7
clay: decorations, 76–7
  frames made using, 81–3
  materials and equipment,
    66–7
  modelling clay, 66, 70
  polymer, 66, 69
coils, wire, 14
copper foil, 11, 30–1

decoupage, 13, 20–1, 24–5

embossing: aluminium foil, 15
  clay, 70
embroidery, 41
equipment see materials and
  equipment

fabrics see silk
felt, 38
  frames made using, 60–1
flowers, artificial, 38
flowers, beadwork, 54–5
flowers, pressed, 38, 42
foil, metal see aluminium foil;
  brass foil; copper foil

glue, 10, 38–9, 66
gutta, metallic, 39

hessian, 39
hooking, rug, 43
interfacing, 39

knives, 38

lead strip, 11
leaves, pressed, 46

materials and equipment:
  fabrics, beads and flowers,
    38–9
  metal, 11
  mosaic, 68
  paper, 10
  plaster and clay, 66–7
medium density fibreboard
  (MDF), 10, 22
metal: frames made using, 11,
  14–15, 30–5
  leaf, 10
mirror frames:
  clay, 78–80
  MDF and wrapping paper,
    22–3
  mosaic, 84–7
  painted tinware, 32–3
  using stones, 90–1
mosaics, 71
  materials and equipment, 68
  mirror frames, 84–7

paper: corrugated, 10, 16
  frames made using, 10, 12–13,
    16–25
  hammered, 19
  pulp, 12, 19
papier mâché, 12, 18

plaster, 66
  frames made using, 72–3
  materials and equipment, 66–7
plastics, 39, 62–3
pliers, 11
poppy seedheads, 44–5
punching, metal, 15, 26–7
raffia, 39
ragwork, 43
ribbonwork, 39, 58–9
rug hooking, 39, 43

sequins, 39, 40, 52–3
shells, 88–9
silk: padded, 56–7
  painted, 39, 40
soldering, 11, 14
stitches, 41
stones: semi-precious, 90–1
string, spirals, 48–9

templates, 92–5
tin: cutting, 15
  painting, 32–3
  plate, 11
  punching, 15, 36–7, 32–3
tin snips (shears), 11
twigs and sticks, 39
twine picture frames, 39

varnishes, 10, 66

wire: making frames using, 11, 14,
  28–9, 34–5